The Sermon on the Mount

A Nondual Interpretation

Marshall Davis

ISBN: 9798857434673

Table of Contents

Did Jesus Really Teach Nonduality? 1

Blessed Emptiness 8

My Lord, What a Mourning! 15

Nondual Awareness as Meekness...............20

Hungry for Rightness........................26

Nondual Mercy...............................32

Purehearted 38

Nondual Peacemaking........................44

Persecuted for Nonduality...................50

Who Does Jesus Say You Are? 57

A Nondual Approach to Scripture 63

The Nondual Ethics of Jesus 69

Nondual Spiritual Practices.................76

The Lord's Prayer – Nondual Style 82

Fasting from Self...........................89

Learning from Nature How to Live 95

Do Not Judge...............................100

How to Enter the Kingdom of God............107

Nondual Discernment 114

How Christianity Lost Its Way..............120

About the Author 127

Other Books by Marshall Davis 129

Did Jesus Really Teach Nonduality?

I am a pastor who proclaims a gospel of Christian nonduality. A few weeks ago I was on a Zoom call with a psychologist who listens to my podcast *The Tao of Christ*. He asked about my nondual interpretation of Jesus' apocalyptic teachings. I began to expound the relevant scripture passages when he interrupted me. He asked, "I understand that this is how you interpret them, but is that what Jesus really meant?" It was an important question, and it began a very interesting conversation about the historical Jesus.

This was not the first time I have been asked a question like this. On another occasion I was being interviewed on a podcast, and the interviewer asked, "Do you REALLY think Jesus taught nonduality?" I could hear the incredulity in his voice. People have a difficult time believing that Jesus really taught nonduality. It is understandable that people would be skeptical of this viewpoint because it is out of the mainstream of Christian thought.

It is hard for people to accept that Jesus was a teacher of nonduality. It is not the typical way of reading Jesus. Some suspect I am reading my own ideas into the words of Jesus. Some Christians accuse me of inserting Eastern religious concepts into the mouth of Jesus. It is a reasonable concern. We all have a tendency to

1

read our own beliefs into a scripture text in order to make it say what we want it to say. It is called eisegesis as opposed to exegesis.

Yet I am convinced that Jesus really taught nonduality. He was not your typical nondual teacher. That may be the reason people resist this approach to the teachings of Jesus. He was not an Adyashanti or Ramana Maharshi. Jesus wasn't a Hindu or a Buddhist. He was a Jew. He came out of Hebrew religion, not Indian religion. His vocabulary and stories reflect his Hebraic heritage.

Furthermore it is not easy for us in the twenty-first century to get into the mind of Jesus. He is separated from us by 2000 years and thousands of miles. It was a different culture in a different time. It is nearly impossible for us to imagine the way that a first century Palestinian Jew in a prescientific age would have thought about the world. For that reason it is extremely difficult to discover the true historical Jesus.

People have been trying to uncover the historical Jesus for centuries. It has been going on in biblical studies for over three hundred years. As an undergrad religion major I read Albert Schweitzer's book entitled *The Quest of the Historical Jesus*, published in 1906. He reviewed the search up to that point, and it has been going on ever since.

Schweitzer concluded that the historical Jesus was an eschatological preacher who believed that the world was coming to an end very soon - within the lifetimes of his listeners.

According to Schweitzer, Jesus proposed an "interim ethic" – a radical ethic of nonviolence, unconditional love and nonjudgment - while he waited for God to bring an end to history.

Since Schweitzer's time scholars have continued the search for the historical Jesus. Scholars have written books seeking to determine exactly what Jesus believed and taught. Was he an apocalyptic preacher? Was he more like a Greek philosopher? Was he a sage, a mystic, a peasant revolutionary, a social reformer, a Pharisaic rabbi, an Essene? There are as many interpretations of Jesus as there are scholars.

In reading these books about Jesus, one common denominator emerges. In the hands of these biblical scholars Jesus's teachings tend to resemble the viewpoint of the authors of the books. If the writer is a Marxist, then Jesus sounds like a Marxist. If the author is a fundamentalist, Jesus sounds like a fundamentalist. If she is a mystic, then Jesus comes off as a mystic. That is a human tendency. Therefore it is reasonable for people to imagine that I am just one more interpreter, twisting Jesus' words to fit my idea of who Jesus was and what he taught.

So did Jesus really teach nonduality? My most direct and honest answer is that we can't be certain what the historical Jesus really thought and taught. This is an historical question, and we do not have sufficient historical evidence to answer that question.

For one thing it is very difficult to determine what the historical Jesus actually said. This is an ongoing question in New Testament scholarship. The famous Jesus Seminar concluded that less than 20% of the words attributed to Jesus in the canonical gospels were actually spoken by him. Most biblical scholars estimate it to be more than that, but we cannot be sure. The truth is we don't know what Jesus really said and how much was put into his mouth by the church to confirm later Christian beliefs. I think it likely that Jesus held a range of beliefs, including but not limited to what we would call nonduality. Some of his teachings were in harmony with nondual teaching, and some were not.

Many of his beliefs reflected his monotheistic Jewish faith. Jesus was a Jew. We cannot turn him into a Buddhist or a Hindu. He was steeped in Hebraic scripture and tradition. He loved to quote the psalms, the Torah and the prophets. He was also influenced by the messianic expectations of his time, which permeated the culture during his lifetime. So it is not surprising that he used messianic and eschatological language.

I try to read Jesus objectively, informed by biblical scholarship and seeking to discern what he really thought and taught. I come to the conclusion that there are two aspects of Jesus. On the one hand Jesus saw himself as a prophet in the tradition of the Old Testament prophets. He described John the Baptist as a prophet and "more than a prophet." Jesus seemed to understand his own role as much the same. Jesus seemed to believe that history was coming to an end in his generation. It was connected in his mind to the destruction of Jerusalem by the Romans.

On the other hand Jesus also sounds like a wisdom teacher, like the wisdom teachers of the Old Testament. He talked about the Kingdom of God here and now, within us and all around us. That aspect of his teaching resonates with nonduality. Jesus combined these two elements. He appeared to think that the already present Kingdom of God was going to be fully manifested in history for all to see in the near future with the destruction of Jerusalem, which happened in 70 AD. That was the theme of a sermon (called the "little apocalypse") that Jesus preached on the Mount of Olives shortly before his death.

If Jesus really believed that history was ending soon, then he was mistaken. It didn't happen. In other words Jesus got it wrong. That is a problem for most Christians. It is difficult for Christians to get their heads around the possibility that Jesus might have been wrong about anything. Christians like to believe Jesus was infallible. It is nearly impossible for evangelical and fundamentalist Christians in particular to accept that Jesus may have been mistaken about something. Yet Jesus admitted that there were some things he did not know and only God knew. Concerning the day of the apocalypse, Jesus said, "But about that day or hour no one knows, not even the angels in heaven, nor the Son, but only the Father."

To suggest that Jesus of Nazareth was not perfect in knowledge is heresy in most Christian circles. Yet the Gospel of Luke says that Jesus "grew in wisdom." In the gospels we read that Jesus would not even accept the word "good" applied to him, much less words like perfect, infallible or inerrant. A young man came up to him and addressed him as "Good teacher," and Jesus retorted, "Why do you call me good? None is good but God alone." That is certainly an authentic saying of Jesus. The church would never put such words into the mouth of Jesus! The later church would prefer to edit that verse out of the canon, but somehow it got through the censors.

Jesus was not infallible, and we should not expect his teachings to be infallible. No spiritual teachers are perfect, nor are their teachings perfect. As I read Jesus, he was a mixture of dualistic notions inherited from his Jewish theistic faith and nondual teachings which he received from his own experience.

Some people speculate that Jesus came in contact with Hindu or Buddhist teachers, either in caravans traveling through the Holy Land or possibly in his own travels to India during the so-called "lost years" of Jesus. In my opinion there is no credible historical evidence to support the claim that Jesus ever traveled to India. Although he may have come in contact with non-Jewish religious and philosophical ideas in Galilee. The so-called "perennial philosophy" was certainly present at that time. More importantly nondual Reality is present at all times and places. Jesus did not need to hear about it from others to experience this reality. In any case his nondual teachings were his unique contributions to the history of Jewish thought.

Many of Jesus' teachings sound like what is called nonduality these days. Not everything Jesus says sounds like nonduality. Yet there is enough to convince me that the core of Jesus' experience of the Kingdom of God and his message of the Kingdom of God was nondual awareness. The Gospel of John focuses on nonduality more than other gospels. In the synoptic gospels, the Sermon on the Mount in Matthew's gospel contains more nondual teachings than other parts of the gospels. The parables lend themselves easily to nondual interpretation as well, and I think that is intentional.

So did Jesus really teach nonduality? Yes, Jesus was a teacher of nonduality. There are certainly other dimensions of his teachings. I will let these parts be proclaimed by others. There are more than enough preachers willing to do that. Yet even these other parts – such as the eschatological and apocalyptic texts - can be interpreted as powerful communicators of nondual truth. I suspect Jesus realized this when he spoke them. In any case this book focuses on the nondual teachings of Jesus, which are the heart of his message and his spirituality.

Blessed Emptiness

Jesus was a teacher of Nonduality. He called it the Kingdom of God. The Sermon on the Mount is the best known and longest sermon by Jesus. So it makes sense that the Sermon on the Mount would be filled with nondual teachings. And it is! Yet this is missed by most Christians because preachers interpret it from the perspective of dualistic theologies rather than nondual awareness. I interpret the Sermon on the Mount as a teaching on nondual Reality.

The sermon begins the Beatitudes. These are eight blessings with a ninth that serves as an epilogue. I call it the Eightfold Path of Jesus. The Buddha had an eightfold path. The Christ had an eightfold path. Their teachings sound different, but that is only because they are products of different cultures - one Indian and one Jewish. Yet they are both pointing to the same Nondual Reality – whether it is called Nirvana or the Kingdom of Heaven.

The Beatitudes get their name from the word that begins each of the verses. In English it is the word blessed. In the Greek language - in which the New Testament was written and possibly the language in which Jesus delivered the sermon - the word is makarios. I need to note here that it is possible that Jesus originally delivered this sermon in his native Aramaic. It is equally possible that as a lifelong resident of "Galilee of the Gentiles," who grew up near

Sepphoris, the Roman administrative center of Galilee and the traditional birthplace of his mother Mary, Jesus delivered this sermon in koine Greek, which was the lingua franca of the region.

The Greek word makarios is normally translated blessed, but sometimes happy. The root of the word, makar, is of ancient non-Greek origin and its root meaning is unknown. We get a hint of its meaning in the Hebrew equivalent used in the Old Testament. In Hebrew it is אֶשֶׁר (esher) and denotes a state of true well-being. If Jesus preached in Aramaic, he would have used the word tubwayhun, which literally means "ripe" or "ready for the picking." It was a word from the agrarian culture Jesus grew up in. When used in reference to people, it can mean integrated, whole, complete, mature. It is not a stretch to say that the Aramaic word points to the wholeness called nonduality.

That is blessedness. One might call it joy, bliss or peace. It is the spiritual quality of unitive awareness or nondual awareness. That means the beatitudes are describing nondual awareness. This word "blessed" is the first word out of the mouth of Jesus in the Sermon on the Mount. It is also the first word of the first psalm in the Book of Psalms. It is likely Jesus did this intentionally, modeling this inaugural teaching after Psalm 1, which is a wisdom psalm.

Jesus began his great sermon saying, "Blessed are the poor in spirit, for theirs is the kingdom of heaven." What does "poor in spirit" mean? The most obvious answer is spiritually

9

poor. That does not make sense in the context of traditional Christianity, but it makes perfect sense in the context of Christian nonduality. To be blessed is to give up everything, not only material things but spiritual things. In regard to material things, it means to live as if one had nothing.

Traditional Christians tend to seek rewards, both material and spiritual. They seek material security on earth and spiritual treasures in heaven. The prosperity gospel folks want to be financially rich as well as spiritually rich! They say you can have it all. That is not historic Christianity. Monastic forms Christianity, for example, take vows of poverty. That is a practice in many spiritual traditions. The Lukan version of this beatitude in the Sermon on the Plain says simply "blessed are the poor" rather than "poor in spirit." Poverty was seen as a blessing of nonattachment to physical things that opened the way for spiritual blessings.

In the Sermon on the Mount Jesus blesses those who are spiritually poor. "Blessed are the poor in spirit." Jesus is teaching nonattachment here. Not only nonattachment to material things but even nonattachment to religious and spiritual rewards. When we have nothing, all barriers are gone and we are everything. Another name for this is emptiness.

The Buddhists call it Śūnyatā, which is normally translated "emptiness," "vacuity," or "voidness." Emptiness is the beginning of nondual awareness. That is why it is mentioned first in Jesus' beatitudes. It is the origin and nature of the universe according to Genesis 1. It says that before creation "The earth was without form and void, and darkness was over the face of the deep." That is symbolic language for nothingness and emptiness. That is how the Torah begins. I think Jesus was basing his sermon on the beginning of the Torah as well as the Psalms.

Jesus is pointing to Emptiness as the original state of the universe, which is our original state and original nature. The first chapter of the Tao Te Ching says, "The nameless is the beginning of heaven and earth. ... Darkness within darkness. The gate to all mystery." I was aware of this Emptiness at the heart of existence many years before I was aware of – and aware as - Nondual Awareness. Experience of this Void was the reason for my venture into existentialism when I was a teenager.

Later when in college Michael Novak visited my college campus promoting his new book *The Experience of Nothingness*, which he described as a common human experience in the West. I remember sitting at his feet in the Student Union listening to him and nodding my head in agreement. I am not recommending his book, but I am saying that the theme resonated with me at the time. It was decades later that I understood this experience of nothingness as the beginning of my journey to nondual awareness. It makes perfect sense to me that this is the beginning of Jesus' teaching on nonduality.

This emptiness is immediately accessible here and now. It feels physically present right behind me as I type these words, impossible to see because I don't have eyes in the back of my head, but always there. This is not nihilistic or depressing in any way. It is just the way it is. It is the deepest level of consciousness. One might even call it the unconscious. To experience this emptiness all we have to do close our eyes and lean back into the void.

This unmanifested Reality is always in the background but is manifested in the foreground. This undifferentiated oneness is manifested in the differentiated diversity of the physical universe. Behind us is the Void. In front of us is the world. Behind us is nothing. In front of us is everything. They are one in the same. Samsara is nirvana. They are one. The fullness of the physical universe is an expression of Emptiness. They are one. We are One.

When one sees everything is Emptiness, then we are poor in spirit. We realize that we own nothing and have nothing and are nothing. That is true freedom. To be poor in spirit is to empty ourselves. In his Letter to the Philippians the apostle Paul quoted an early Christian hymn that describes Jesus as emptying himself, and he proposes this approach as a model for us. He wrote: "Let this mind be in you which was also in Christ Jesus, who, being in the form of God, did not consider it robbery to be equal with God, but emptied Himself...." This is known as kenosis in Christian theology. John of the Cross talks about self-emptying a lot.

Those who empty themselves of everything - including themselves - are returning to their true Self. They rid themselves of everything that is not them, and they realize that in reality we are nothing. This is the Via Negativa of Christian mysticism. This is the process of deconstruction. In this process we deconstruct everything we have been taught by our family, society and religion about who we are. When we empty ourselves of all ideas, labels and assumptions, we see what we really are. It is like waking up from drunkenness. We have been intoxicated with things and drunk with ideas about ourselves. Getting rid of all of our mental baggage is what Jesus meant by "poor in spirit."

The author of Ecclesiastes was saying this when he started off his book with the words, "Emptiness, Emptiness, All is emptiness." The traditional wording is "vanity, vanity, all is vanity." The Hebrew word is hebel, which is more accurately translated emptiness or nothingness. The central theme of Ecclesiastes is the Buddhist teaching of impermanence. Jesus may have had those opening words of Ecclesiastes in mind in his opening words of the Sermon on the Mount. Jesus was echoing the opening words of several biblical books with his opening words. So many ancient texts point to this emptiness as the beginning of the wisdom of knowing nondual reality.

This not an idea to accept. If it is only an idea to be added to our collection of spiritual ideas in our worldview it is worthless. This is emptiness of all ideas. This emptiness is experienced by intuition, going behind the mind to the existential reality that is the nature of everything. "All is emptiness!" Ecclesiastes says. Noticing this emptiness is the first step in awakening to nondual awareness. This is the Kingdom of Heaven according to Jesus.

My Lord, What a Mourning!

The beatitudes are the eightfold path of Jesus. They are eight blessings that introduce Jesus' famous Sermon on the Mount. They all describe what is called nondual awareness. The second beatitude says, "Blessed are those who mourn, for they shall be comforted." This is usually interpreted by Christian preachers as having to do with the familiar phenomenon of grief. We cannot get too far along in life without significant loss, including the death of loved ones. The grieving process applies not only to the death of people, but also divorce, losing a beloved pet or friendship or a job or a home or one's health or many other situations.

This common type of grief is an important aspect of life, but this is not what Jesus is talking about in his beatitude. Jesus is speaking in the context of nonduality. The Way of nonduality involves grief. It involves mourning. People often assume that spiritual awakening brings an instant end to all the problems of life. The truth is that awakening begins with a grief of its own before it blossoms into comfort that ends suffering. This is what Jesus is talking about when he says, "Bless are those who mourn, for they shall be comforted."

Spiritual awakening involves the loss of all things, including the self. That loss brings grief. Jesus repeatedly said that to follow him meant giving up everything. He said, "Whoever seeks to save his life shall lose it, and whoever loses his life shall find it." The spiritual life involves loss and therefore grief. Jesus specifically listed family. "Anyone who loves his father or mother more than me is not worthy of me; anyone who loves his son or daughter more than me is not worthy of me; and anyone who does not take up his cross and follow me is not worthy of me." Awakening to our true nature means the loss of our old self and everything associated with it.

About a year ago I was talking to a man who was reluctant to pursue spiritual awakening because he thought it would be the end of emotion. He was afraid that spiritual awakening would be akin to an emotional lobotomy. He was concerned that he would feel nothing. He asked me if I still felt emotions. I assured him that feelings are still present. They are an integral part of the body and the mind, and they remain as long as the body and mind are alive. The difference is that one knows that emotional and mental states are not who we are. They are phenomena that are just passing through the body, like storms passing through the countryside. I am not the body or mind, so there is no attachment to mental states. That is comfort. That is peace. He was unconvinced.

When one sees that one is not a separate self, then we lose everything that was associated with the separate self. Yet we gain much more. We gain everything. We lose mortal life but gain eternal life. One is not an individual self; one is the One True Self manifested in all eight billion souls that are present on earth now. So one loses and grieves one individual life, but gains eight billion lives. Thus we feel compassion for these 8 billion people, which means we share in their lives. We suffer with those who suffer and rejoice with those who rejoice. Our emotional life is far richer than before.

That is what Jesus was talking about a few chapters later when he says, "And everyone who has left houses or brothers or sisters or father or mother or wife or children or fields for the sake of My name will receive a hundredfold and will inherit eternal life." In context he is saying that this happens at what he calls "the renewal of all things." That is typically pictured as an apocalyptic event in the future, but that is linear thinking. In reality there is no future or past. Those are categories of the mind. The Kingdom of God is here. The renewal of all things is now.

So, yes, we lose everything that we thought we were and had, and we grieve that loss. Jesus felt that grief in the Garden of Gethsemane as he prepared to die on the cross. Jesus was emotional. In anticipating this loss of life, there was grief. There was mourning. Yet it was swallowed up by the joy of surrender to what is, and thereby we gain everything.

There is an African American spiritual entitled "My Lord, What a Mourning," which talks about the renewal of all things that Jesus was talking about. The lyrics are:

My Lord, what a mourning,
My Lord, what a mourning,
Oh, my Lord, what a mourning
When the stars begin to fall.

In most hymnals the word is spelled *morning*, in the sense of the beginning of the day. But in a hymnal that we used in one of my churches it was spelled with a u - *mourning*, meaning grieving. My Lord, what a mourning! What a grieving! I researched the history of this hymn and discovered that this was the original spelling in the earliest published version of this hymn. The song was first printed in the book *Slave Songs* published in 1867. It spells it "mournin.' This interpretation has scriptural support in Jesus' little apocalypse given on the Mount of Olives, when he says "then all the tribes of the earth will mourn."

Both spellings have merit. Death precedes rebirth. Mourning precedes the morning. As the psalm says, "Those who sow with tears will reap with songs of joy." This is the truth behind Jesus' words, "Blessed are those who mourn, for they shall be comforted." Jesus may have had the psalm in mind. Jesus loved the Psalms and quoted from them.

When one deconstructs one's present life, that process involves grief. I experienced grief firsthand during those years I was deconstructing my Christianity from 2009 to 2011. I was grieving the loss of my religion and the worldview that I had known all my adult life. We grieve when we discover that reality is not what we thought it was and that we are not what we thought we were. But the grief turns to joy when the falsehoods and the false self fall away and we see clearly what and who we really are. That is a rebirth.

The spiritual life involves death. That is the meaning of the cross. With the deaths come mourning. The good news is that we are comforted by the realization that death is swallowed up in victory. That is the meaning of the resurrection. We see that we are not ever separate from one another or separate from God. We are all one in God. All are one in Christ. When one sees that, then grief is turned to comfort. "Blessed are those who mourn for they shall be comforted." That is the blessing of unitive awareness.

Nondual Awareness as Meekness

In this chapter we look at the third beatitude in Jesus' eightfold path of nondual awareness: "Blessed are the meek, for they shall inherit the earth." To understand this saying we must know what he means by meek. This is a badly misunderstood word because of the common association of meekness with weakness. Meekness is not weakness. It is the exact opposite. The Torah describes Moses as meek. "Now the man Moses was very meek, more than all people who were on the face of the earth." Yet he was champion of the Hebrew people, a prince of Egypt who lead a rebellion against Pharaoh and freed the people of Israel from slavery, a story celebrated by the Jews every Passover.

So meek does not mean weak. When I think of meek I think of someone like Mahatma Gandhi, who appeared to be a harmless little man in a loincloth. Yet he freed his country from the British Empire in a nonviolent revolution. Meek is not weak. Ramana Maharshi was another little man in a loincloth. Jesus was meek but not weak, even though he also advocated nonviolence. The Buddha was meek. Thomas Merton was meek. Great spiritual leaders tend to be meek, but they are certainly not weak.

The best definition of meek is selfless. Meekness is selflessness. I am not using that word in the common sense of the opposite of selfish, but in the nondual sense of being without self. Spiritual awakening opens us up to see that we are not a self. We do not have a self. We are literally self-less. Jesus saw through the facade of the personal self at his spiritual awakening, which happened at his baptism at the Jordan River. It transformed his life from being an unknown small town carpenter to being a great spiritual leader that changed history.

Once Jesus saw through the illusion of the individual self, he was open to the Universal Self. Once he shed his separate identity he knew his divine identity. In Christian lingo, he was filled with the Holy Spirit, baptized in the Spirit of God, Divine Reality. Meekness is selflessness. Selflessness is the definition of nonduality.

In nondual awareness it is seen that there is One Self, one Reality. It is seen that there is no inside or outside. We tend to think of ourselves as separate psychological entities residing inside fleshly bodies that are different from the outside world. In spiritual awakening the barrier between inside and outside, us and them, me and the other, dissolves. It is seen that all is One. We are the All.

Southernmost is a novel by Silas House. It is about a Pentecostal pastor in Tennessee who has a crisis of faith that upends his position as a pastor, his marriage, and his family. The story centers on the issue of accepting LGBTQ people into the church. Besides the preacher, the other main character is his nine year-old son Justin. Even though Justin has been raised in a very conservative church, he has an untraditional spirituality. In a chapter entitled "The Everything" there is a description of this nine-year-old's understanding of God. Here is the opening paragraph of that chapter, which takes place in the Florida Keys:

> *Justin used to think the trees were God. But today, right here, he thinks the ocean might be God. All that power and weakness, spread out for us to see. The ocean can do so much when it wants to, and sometimes it can do nothing but go in and out, waves and smoothness. The ocean is a mystery and so is God. They are both so big we cannot see all of them at the same time but we can catch pieces of them here and there. Justin believes God is big like the ocean. Even bigger. But lots of people don't. They think He's small enough to fit in a church house or an offering plate or an ancient book.*

Later in this chapter are these words:

> *This is the kind of talk that would horrify his mother, but he believes God is in everything and everybody. Pieces of him. He doesn't just mean the spirit, he means the actual chunks of God. He thinks He's not only in the ocean, but also in Shady, [Shady is a stray dog they pick up and adopt on the trip from Tennessee to Florida] and the sand, and the trees, and every person on this beach, every person in the world. Today, right this minute, Justin can see nothing but ocean, and that is Everything. And Justin can feel the*

Everything beneath his hand where he is resting his palm on Shady's chest and Shady's heart thrums in a steady rhythm like the waves on the beach. He can feel the Everything under himself in the gritty sand. He can smell it in the seaweedy smell smoothing over his face. He can hear it in the laughter of the teenagers down the beach and in the crying of that baby and the metal sound of the airplane sliding over them all and the water coming in and out in and out. The ocean is God but so are we all.

Everything is God. Elsewhere this novel quotes Thomas Merton, who was an early influence in my life during college. Merton said, "Everything that is, is holy." William Blake famously said, "Everything that lives is holy."

I wrote a blog post a year ago entitled "Everything is Holy Now." I was reflecting on a memorial service I attended online for Fran Bennett, who was a nondual teacher and also transgender. At the service the song "Holy Now" by Peter Mayer was played. It was a song she often sang at her retreats. It echoes the spiritual awakening she experienced in 2010 while taking the Eucharist. The first stanza says:

When I was a boy, each week
On Sunday, we would go to church
And pay attention to the priest.
He would read the holy word
And consecrate the holy bread
And everyone would kneel and bow.
Today the only difference is

Everything is holy now.
Everything, everything,
Everything is holy now.

In my blog post I wrote these words: "Everyone is holy. My transgender friend Fran was – and is – holy. My friend David was my roommate in college and a groomsman in my wedding. He was gay, a seminary-educated ordained Unitarian Universalist minister, a lifelong friend, and one of the best people I have known. He ended his earthly life twenty years ago because the anti-gay hate of our culture was more than his sensitive soul could bear. Everyone is holy. Everything is holy."

Those words prompted an angry response from one of my closest friends, who is a devout Calvinist. In recent years he has become much more legalistic and intolerant, following the trend of evangelicalism. In an email he accused me of all sorts of heresies. All because I would not judge people, which is what Jesus taught us to do! The beatitudes tells us to expect this type of reaction. Jesus said, "Blessed are you when they revile and persecute you, and say all kinds of evil against you falsely for My sake."

In his email my friend argued "If everything is holy, nothing is holy." I responded, "If everything is not holy, nothing is holy." This is the difference between traditional theism and the spirituality of Jesus. The Pharisees were theists and saw everything in terms of black and white, holy and unholy. They saw themselves as holy and others as not holy.

Many Christians think in this dualistic way today. Jesus erases this distinction. Jesus fellowshipped with outsiders, whom religious people called sinners and unclean; he said these "sinners" were entering the Kingdom of God ahead of the Pharisees. The gospel says that at Jesus' death the veil of the Holy of holies was torn in two from top to bottom. This powerful symbolic action means that everything is now holy – not just a few square feet in the Temple, but everywhere and everything and everyone, not just a chosen people.

That is what Jesus meant when he said that the meek inherit the earth. Jesus said in the Gospel of Thomas that one who sees the Truth will rule over "the All." He says, "Let him who seeks continue seeking until he finds. When he finds, he will become troubled. When he becomes troubled, he will be astonished, and he will rule over the All." That is what Jesus means when he says that the meek shall inherit the earth.

Jesus did not intend for his followers to rule over a political, military kingdom on earth - a Christian nation, run by Christian laws and defended by Christian soldiers marching to the tune of "Onward Christian Soldiers." Jesus rejected that temptation of the devil in the wilderness during the 40 days after his baptism/spiritual awakening. Jesus meant that the meek are those who have awakened to the truth that the whole world is yours, and you are world's, and All is one. "Blessed are the meek, for they shall inherit the earth."

Hungry for Rightness

The fourth of Jesus' nondual beatitudes says, "Blessed are those who hunger and thirst for righteousness, for they will be satisfied." This may be the most important of the eight beatitudes. At least it has been most important in my life. It is the one consistent characteristic of my search for truth. It eventually resulted in the shift that is called spiritual awakening.

Since the time I was a teenager I have had a hunger for truth. I needed to know the ultimate truth of the universe. It is what led me to become a religion major in college, long before I considered myself a Christian. I entered college planning to be a scientist, a geologist to be specific. I loved geology. I think it was because of all the time I spent hiking in the White Mountains of New Hampshire as a youth. The power that is able to transform the landscape, push up and erode down mountains, and move continents fascinated me. I wanted to study it.

I took a geology class in high school, and I was hooked. I entered college intent on becoming a geologist, and so I immediately declared myself as a geology major. I also was taking religion courses to feed a spiritual hunger in me. In a couple of years my spiritual hunger overcame my scientific interest.

I still vividly remember the reaction of my academic advisor, who was also the head of the geology department, when I told him I was switching majors from geology to religion. He asked me why, and I responded that I wanted something practical. He was dumbstruck. He could not fathom how religion could be more practical than geology! For me it was obvious. Religion held the possibility of knowing the meaning of the universe. What could be more important or more practical than that?

I hungered and thirsted for the truth behind the universe. In time that hunger and thirst blossomed into spiritual awakening, or what Jesus called "eternal life." That is the meaning behind the beatitude "Blessed are those who hunger and thirst for righteousness, for they will be satisfied." I am satisfied. No more searching. No more wondering.

To know what Jesus meant by this beatitude, we have to understand what is meant by the term righteousness. This is where a lot of Christians go astray. The term righteousness has been colored by a legalistic interpretation of the term. This is due to the influence of the apostle Paul, who was a Pharisee. In spite of his conversion, the apostle Paul remained a Pharisee at heart. He never could jettison his legalistic worldview which saw relationship with God in terms of the Law.

He saw humans as condemned sinners standing before the Judge of the universe - sinners in the hands of an angry God, to use Jonathan Edwards' phrase. Paul set out to solve this problem using the death of Jesus as the transactional solution to a cosmic legal problem. He saw Jesus' death as a propitiation, an atoning sacrifice that satisfied the Law. Christianity has been following his pattern ever since. That is the problem with Christianity. It listens to Paul more than Jesus. Christians read the Pharisaic interpretation of righteousness into Jesus' beatitude.

Jesus did not see righteousness in that way. Jesus never suggested that his death had such a meaning. He was not a Pharisee or a Torah lawyer. In fact the Pharisees were his greatest critics. Jesus was more like the prophets or the wisdom teachers of the Old Testament. That is why it is ironic that the religion that bears his name is so pharisaical.

To properly understand the intimidating word "righteousness," all we have to do is take the long ending off the word. At its root it simply means right. Righteousness is rightness. It is when everything is seen as right. Everything is right with the world and the universe. We are right with the universe. It is no accident that the Buddha's Noble Eightfold path also uses the word "right" repeatedly: Right View, Right Resolve, Right Speech, Right Action, Right Livelihood, Right Effort, Right Mindfulness, and Right Concentration. Both Jesus and Buddha talk about rightness.

People intuitively sense that things are not right. That is what the Buddha meant when he said that life is dukkha. The word means out of kilter, off balance, not right. This is the source of the existential angst of the West. The Bible calls this condition sin – not individual sins but the state of sin – sin-ness. People sense that something is wrong. They seek rightness. Religions concoct all sorts of systems to set things right, but the simple truth is that rightness is here now, if we simply reach out our hand. In Jesus' words, "The Kingdom of God is at hand.

When Jesus uses the word righteousness, he is talking about this rightness. Rightness is when there is no distinction between what is and the way we want it to be. They are one. This acceptance of reality as it is now, is faith. It is the surrender voiced by Jesus in Gethsemane when he said, "Not my will but thine be done." Suffering comes from expecting things to be different than they are.

So this beatitude is paradoxical. People hunger and thirst for a spiritual reality that is actually already present. People just don't realize it. By proclaiming this gospel I am selling water by the river, as the Zen saying puts it. People hunger and thirst for something we think we do not have. Only when we exhaust all possibilities and come up empty do we give up the search and discover that we had access to this treasure all along. With this realization we are full. We are satisfied.

Rightness surpasses relationship. Sometimes Christians describe righteousness as right relationship with God, but relationship implies duality. There has to be two to have a relationship. Jesus' understanding of rightness transcends relationship. Rightness is being one with Reality, one with God, union with God. That is what Jesus prayed for his followers to know in his prayer in the Garden of Gethsemane. Union with God is very different from being in a relationship with God. Jesus said, "I and the Father are one." He wants that awareness of oneness for us.

To hunger and thirst for righteousness is to desire rightness more than anything else, to desire it until the desire exhausts itself and drops away and there is only God. We cannot manufacture this hunger and thirst. It is grace. The only problem is that most people do not hunger for this. Because of that they are never satisfied. They do not make this a priority in their lives. For many people spirituality is a side gig. It is one aspect of life alongside many other parts – like work or family or romance or recreation or whatever. Spirituality is simply one facet of their self-image.

For Jesus everything was about the Kingdom of God. He had a zeal for God that consumed him. That is how the gospel writer described Jesus in the story about the cleansing of the temple. Spiritual awakening requires single-minded determination. That is what the Buddha was pointing to with his list of eight rights. To hunger and thirst for rightness is the meaning of the fourth beatitude.

The following story has many forms, but because I am a Baptist preacher I like the Baptist version. A young man came to a preacher and said he wanted eternal life. The preacher asked if he really wanted it, and the man assured the clergyman that he really did. So the preacher said he would take him down to the river and baptize him – by immersion of course. The preacher took that man into the river and dunked him under. But instead of immediately bringing him up from the water, he held him under.

He held him under until the man was afraid he was going to drown. The man kicked, flailed his arms, hit the preacher, and did everything he could to get out of the water. When the preacher finally let go of him, the man came up sputtering and coughing and spitting up river water. After he caught his breath, he yelled at the preacher, "What are you trying to do, kill me?" The preacher responded, "You said you wanted eternal life. When you want eternal life as much as you wanted a breath of air a moment ago, then you will find eternal life."

When we hunger and thirst for rightness the way a drowning man wants air or a starving man wants food or a thirsty man wants water, then we find what we are looking for. "Blessed are those who hunger and thirst for righteousness, for they will be satisfied."

Nondual Mercy

The fifth of the eight nondual beatitudes of Jesus says, "Blessed are the merciful, for they shall receive mercy." The word "merciful" literally means full of mercy. It describes how we relate to others. At first hearing that may sound dualistic. Relating to others is by nature dualistic. All relationships presuppose at least two parties. That means duality. For that reason some people think nonduality has nothing to say about relationships.

Some people seeking liberation from this dualistic world avoid relationships, and focus exclusively on the interior life. That is the whole point of becoming an ascetic. Even Jesus' disciples left family to follow Jesus. Jesus left his family. So did the Buddha. So did a lot of spiritual leaders.

Many sincere spiritual seekers have gone off by themselves and lived alone in the forest or in a cave. There is a long tradition in both India and the Middle East, both in Hinduism and in Christianity (I am thinking of the desert fathers and mothers in Egypt) of people becoming wandering ascetics or hermits in order to avoid relationships and focus on salvation or liberation.

Yet there is an equally strong tradition of living the spiritual life in community. Buddhists take refuge in the sangha. Christians have the church. The fact is humans need other people. It is how we evolved as a species. People have tried to strike a balance by surrounding themselves with like-minded, spiritually-minded people, whether that is in monasteries, ashrams, sectarian churches, religious communities or other types of intentional communities.

Most of us will find ourselves surrounded by other people, and they are not obstacles to the spiritual life. Yet we need to know how to relate to people in a way consistent with nondual reality. Even though we know that we are all one Divine Self, we find ourselves relating to other ego selves. That the nature of human life. The question becomes how to live an authentic life that expresses nondual reality in the midst of dualistic relationships.

That is what this beatitude is about. Part of the nondual lifestyle – if you want to call it that - is to be merciful. Blessed are the merciful. Mercy is related to the Buddhist virtue of compassion. The Buddha was compassionate. The Christ was merciful. They are two facets of the same gem. In fact the eight beatitudes could be pictured as an eight-faced gem called an octahedron.

To be merciful means not to condemn. It means not to judge. Jesus deals with this later in the Sermon on the Mount, when he says, "Judge not, lest you be judged." Jesus said in full: "Do not judge, or you too will be judged. For in the same way you judge others, you will be judged, and with the measure you use, it will be measured to you." That is just another way of saying, "Blessed are the merciful, for they shall receive mercy."

What is the source of this mercy? The source of mercy is nondual awareness. Mercy comes from firsthand knowledge that we are one with the other. We extend mercy to others because we are the other. We love our neighbor as ourselves because we see that our neighbor is our self. Our neighbor is literally the Self, and so we love them as ourselves. We love our enemies because we see that our enemy is us. "We have met the enemy and he is us," as Pogo said.

Most traditional Christians do not get this. Traditional Christianity has strayed from Jesus' original nondual teaching and become dualistic. They see the world in terms of us and them. Everything is black and white – believers and nonbelievers, the saved and the lost, heaven or hell, saints and sinners, good and evil, righteous and unrighteous, on and on. For that reason Christianity has historically been prone to demonize people who think and act differently than they do. They demonize the adherents of other religions, even calling them demon-worshippers.

Christians think they are the only ones going to heaven because they live within a dualistic worldview. For that reason they have a difficult time with mercy. Their concept of mercy is very limited and dualistic. They picture God as a Judge who condemns his enemies and consigns them to eternal hell while ushering Christians into a celestial paradise. Mercy, as far as traditional Christianity understands it, is extended only to true Christian believers who meet the right standards, involving doctrine, morals, beliefs, and rituals. Only those who qualify are eligible for mercy, according to them.

But mercy by definition is not for those who "deserve" it, but for those who do not deserve it. Otherwise it is not mercy. That means it is for everyone or no one. Likewise the merciful open their hearts to everyone. Mercy is breaking down barriers between us and the other. There is no us and other in mercy. There are not two. There is only one. Mercy is at heart nondual. Mercy is unconditional. If it were not, it would not be mercy!

The prime example of mercy in the ministry of Jesus is the gospel story of the woman caught in adultery. The title and situation of the story is sexist because it pictures men judging a woman. If the woman in the story was caught in adultery, as her accusers said, that means there was a man committing adultery with her. Where is he? If she had committed adultery with another woman, then you can be sure there would have been two woman dragged into the temple and brought before Jesus!

You cannot commit adultery by yourself. Yet the man who committed adultery with her is not presented before the crowd to be stoned to death, only the woman. You can be certain that the man received mercy, but the woman did not! She was going to be judged to the fullest extent of the law.

The scene takes place in the temple courts. Some Pharisees and teachers of the Law drag this woman before Jesus, and say, "Teacher, this woman was caught in the act of adultery. The Law of Moses says to stone her. What do you say?" The narrator goes on to explain that they were trying to trap Jesus into saying something that they could use against him.

But Jesus "never said a mumblin' word," as the African American spiritual puts it. He just doodles in the dust with his finger while thinking how to respond. They keep demanding an answer, so finally he stands and says, "Let him without sin cast the first stone!" Then he goes back to doodling in the sand.

This is the turning point in the story. Each of the accusers silently drop their stones and walk away, beginning with the oldest. Eventually only Jesus and the woman are left. He stands, looks around him, and says to the woman, "Where are your accusers? Didn't even one of them condemn you?" "No, Lord," she said. Jesus said, "Neither do I. Go and sin no more."

Jesus showed mercy. He did it in a way that demonstrated to her accusers that they were no different from the woman. That is the message of nonduality. We are no different from anyone else. When we see ourselves in others, then we are merciful to others. "Blessed are the merciful, for they shall receive mercy."

Some preachers make a big deal of that fact that Jesus told the woman, "Go and sin no more." They say, "See, Jesus is calling her a sinner." The ego of these male preachers still wants to judge this woman as a sinner. They have to let her go this time because Jesus said so, but they are just waiting for her to sin again, so they can stone her to death. For them mercy means two strikes and you're out. Such an attitude completely misses Jesus' point. Jesus is dramatically teaching religious leaders not to judge, but to extend mercy.

"Blessed are the merciful, for they shall receive mercy." The beatitude is equally true in reverse, "Blessed are those who have received mercy, for they are merciful." When we have experienced the unconditional mercy of God, then it is naturally expressed in the way we treat others. We are merciful when the crowd is not merciful. We are expressions of nondual mercy in an unmerciful world.

Purehearted

In the sixth beatitude Jesus describes nondual awareness as pureheartedness. He says, "Blessed are the pure in heart, for they shall see God." At the present time I am rereading the Ashtavakra Gita, which is one of the classics of Indian nondualism. The author talks about "pure in heart" in chapter 17. "The liberated soul abides in the Self alone and is pure of heart." That gives a hint as to what Jesus is talking about when he says, "Blessed are the pure in heart, for they shall see God."

Using similar language Jesus, speaking as the Divine Self, says, "Abide in me and I in you." When we abide in the True Nature, the separate self dissipates and the Divine Self shines through. We are transparent to the presence of God. The smog of the ego clears, and we see God.

Webster's Dictionary defines purehearted as "having the heart free from guile." That describes the disciple Nathanael. In the beginning of the Gospel of John Jesus is gathering disciples. He called Philip, who immediately went and told his friend Nathanael about Jesus of Nazareth. Nathanael responds, "Can anything good come out of Nazareth?" Philip replied, "Come and see." Jesus saw Nathanael coming toward Him, and said, "Behold, an Israelite in whom there is no guile!" In other words Nathanael was purehearted. Nathanael's response is: "Rabbi,

You are the Son of God!" He saw God in Jesus because he was pure of heart.

Pure of heart means to be transparent, to be able to see through the illusion of dualistic existence to nondual Divinity. The lake near our home in New Hampshire is very clear. The water quality is classified as "pristine." You can swim out far, and see the sandy bottom of lake clearly because it is so transparent. That is what it means to be pure of heart. You can look into the depths of the heart and see the bottom. At the bottom of the human heart is God, the Ground of Being. That is what it means: "Blessed are the pure in heart, for they shall see God."

What if one's heart does not seem very clear? What if we cannot see to the bottom of the soul and see God? Sometimes on busy days the water of our lake is stirred up by motor boats, so that we cannot see to the bottom. The Tao Te Ching talks about letting water settle until it is clear. Lao Tzu says, "Who can make the muddy water clear? Let it be still, and it will gradually become clear." In "The Way of Zen" Alan Watts wrote: "Muddy water is best cleared by leaving it alone."

There is a Buddhist story that illustrates this. Buddha and his disciples were on a journey and came to a lake. Buddha said to his youngest and most impatient disciple: "I'm thirsty. Please bring me some water from that lake." The disciple went to the lake, but when he arrived a wagon of oxen was crossing it. As they stirred up the silt, the water became cloudy. The disciple thought, "I can't give the teacher this muddy water to drink." So he went back and told

Buddha, "The water is very muddy, I don't think we can drink it."

After about a half an hour later, Buddha asked the disciple to go back to the lake and bring him some water to drink. The disciple went again, but the water was still dirty. Once again he returned and said to Buddha: "We can't drink that water. We should walk to the town to get something to drink." Buddha didn't answer. However, he didn't make any movement to leave either. He just stayed there.

After a while longer, the Buddha asked the disciple again to go back to the lake and bring him water. As he didn't want to challenge his master, he went to the lake. When he arrived, he observed that the water now looked crystal clear. He collected some water and brought it to Buddha, who looked at it and said to the disciple, "What have you done to clean the water?" The disciple didn't understand the question, for he hadn't done anything.

The Buddha explained, "You waited and let it be. Therefore the silt settled on its own and now the water is clear. Your mind is like that! When it's cloudy, you simply need to let it be. Give it some time. It'll clear on its own. You don't have to make any effort to calm it down. Everything will clear on its own as long as you don't bother it." What is true of the mind is true of the heart as well.

That may sound like inaction, but it is not. It is wei wu wei, as the Tao Te Ching puts it. Action without action. As McCartney sang, "Let it be. Let it be. Let it be. Let it be. There will be an answer. Let it be." That is the reality behind all eight of the beatitudes. Jesus is not urging us to do anything in these eight blessings. He is not issuing a set of commandments or instructions. He is not saying "Thou shalt not" or "Thou shalt." He says simply "Blessed is." He is pronouncing blessings on those who are who they are.

The dualistic world is very action oriented. That attitude seeps into religion and spirituality. People want to do something to achieve a spiritual goal. Seekers want to do something to be enlightened or awakened. The rich young man came to Jesus asking, "Good teacher, what must I do to inherit eternal life?" He does not see the contradiction in his request. One does not have to do anything to inherit. One inherits because of who one is, not what one does. Inheritance is a gift, not a work. It is a birthright.

One does not do anything to be pure in heart or to see God. One does nothing, and yet all is accomplished. All one does is abide. Jesus says, "Abide in me and I in you." He uses the metaphor of the vine and the branch. The branch does not make an effort to produce fruit. It simply abides in the vine. The psalmist says, "Be still and know that I am God." All one has to do is be still, abide in God. Wei wu wei. When one acts without acting, the muddy water clears and one can see to the bottom of the soul. One sees God. Nothing has changed. The only difference is that one sees what one did not see before.

This beatitude is not an instruction to engage in countless hours of meditation in order to accomplish the goal of clearing the mind. This is not about training the mind to have no thoughts. Thoughts will be with us always. Emotions will always be present. It is not a matter of trying to get rid of them. Just let them be, and they will quiet down. Even if they never quiet down, God is still the root of the soul. It is not about changing anything. It is about seeing what does not change. That is what Nathanael saw when he listened to Jesus. He did not see Jesus of Nazareth; he saw through the man and saw God.

Christians sometimes retort that the Bible says that one cannot see God. Earlier in this same chapter in the Gospel of John, the author writes, "No one has ever seen God." There is the well-known statement in the Torah where God says to Moses, "You cannot see my face, for no one can see me and live." This does not contradict the beatitude. It is the whole point of the beatitude! Being pure of heart means to be no one. No one can see God. Only when one is no one, can one see God. When one sees that one is not a self, then one can see the Self.

The human sense of an individual self gets in the way of seeing God. The ego is the dirt that muddies the water. The separate self clouds the mind and heart. It prevents us from seeing what we are and prevents us from seeing God. When that self settles to the bottom of human consciousness, then we can see clearly. We see God.

When the Bible says that no one can see God and live, it is saying that the separate self cannot exist in the presence of the Divine Self. When the prophet Isaiah saw God, his response was, "Woe is me. I am undone! For my eyes have seen the King, the Lord of hosts!" He felt like he was coming undone.

I had the same experience as Isaiah. In the presence of God I had the sense of dissolving, disintegrating, returning to dust and ashes. I was not, and it scared me (the small self) to death. So much so that I ran from the presence of God like Jonah. I hid from God for twenty years inside evangelical Christianity until I could hide no more. I discovered that Christianity is a good place to hide from God. A lot of people hide from God there. But only for so long. Finally God strips away the hiding places. Then all is clear. Then one sees God.

Nondual Peacemaking

The seventh of the nondual beatitudes of Jesus says, "Blessed are the peacemakers, for they shall be called children of God." Unitive awareness is characterized by peace. Inner peace that promotes outer peace. This is the peace that passes human understanding. It is the peace of God, the peace of Christ, the Prince of peace.

It is a different type of peace than the dualistic world knows. Jesus famously said, "Peace I leave with you. My peace I give unto you. Not as the world gives, do I give to you. Let not your heart be troubled, neither let it be afraid." That is my wife's favorite verse. She often quotes it, shares it often, and it has seen her through a lot.

The peace of Christ is holistic peace. It is wholeness, oneness. It is peace that knows from experience that there is no division or separation between us and God, between us and others, or between us and the world. All is one in perfect peace. This is not a belief or a conviction; it is known directly.

It is the peace that comes from realizing that everything is right exactly as it is now. There is nothing that has to be changed. It doesn't seem like that when seen through dualistic eyes. It seems like the world is going to hell in a handbasket. Yet peace is present now, if we have eyes to see. Yet people do not see. That is why nonduality expresses itself in peacemaking. "Blessed are the peacemakers, for they shall be called children of God."

The dualistic world of appearances does not know peace. It is always at war with itself. Opposites are battling on the world stage. These wars come from the battle in the human psyche. Politics is a social expression of the psyche. Nothing could be more dualistic than the two major American political parties, especially in their current extreme incarnations. These two forces are tearing our nation apart. In New Hampshire we have the first presidential primary in the nation. It is all grassroots campaigning. I get the opportunity to personally hear, speak with, and shake hands with (if I want to) every person running for president. It is a great spectator sport!

As a result it is easy to get sucked into this dualistic political battle. It is easy to see the two parties and the two sides in terms of a battle between good and evil, right and wrong. Nonduality shows us the wholeness that is beyond good and evil.

Culture wars are depicted by both sides as a battle between good and evil. The right wing and the left wing both see themselves as the good guys and the other side as evil. This model fits right into traditional Christianity, which sees the world as a battleground between God and Satan. When we demonize our enemies and don haloes for ourselves, then we are immersed in duality and blind to nondual reality.

Nonduality transcends good and evil, right and wrong. In unitive awareness everything and everyone is an expression of God. Nondual reality is expressed in both good and evil. There are indications of this in the Bible. Who planted the tree of the knowledge of good and evil in the Garden of Eden according to Genesis? It was the theistic God! Who created the serpent, which is the symbol for evil in Genesis? It was the theistic God. So this nondual truth is present in nascent form even in biblical theism.

In the Book of Isaiah God says, "I am the LORD, and there is none else. I form the light, and create darkness. I make peace, and create evil. I the LORD do all these things." That inclusive God is very different from the dualistic deity who is only light. "God is light an in him there is no darkness at all," says the first epistle of John. Much of the Bible is dualistic, but there are those rare texts that point to a deeper truth. Nondual awareness sees the peace that is behind the opposing forces of good and evil, right and wrong, light and darkness. It sees the wholeness that includes both yin and yang.

So how is this lived out in our human lives? In the previous chapter about being pure of heart, I quoted Alan Watts, who said, "Muddy water is best cleared by leaving it alone." That is only part of the quote from his book, *The Way of Zen*. The full quote says this: "Furthermore, as muddy water is best cleared by leaving it alone, it could be argued that those who sit quietly and do nothing are making one of the best possible contributions to a world in turmoil."

That is nondual peacemaking. We live in a world that thinks that the only way to accomplish change is through dualistic action, good fighting evil. Where has that brought us? Where does that get us in American politics? Both right and left think they are good and are fighting evil. As the fight goes on, they are lured into thinking that their goals must be reached by any means possible – by any candidate available. Soon the ends justify the means, and the good guys become indistinguishable from the bad guys.

People who are not actively engaged in this battle between relative good and evil are considered irrelevant. That is why politics has taken over evangelical Christianity in the US. But Watts says, "it could be argued that those who sit quietly and do nothing are making one of the best possible contributions to a world in turmoil." Perhaps those who pray and meditate are doing more for peace than all the politicians, statesmen and soldiers in the world.

Watts goes on in the book to say, "Yet it should be obvious that action without wisdom, without clear awareness of the world as it really is, can never improve anything." The key phrase is "clear awareness of the world as it really is." He is talking about nondual awareness. The best thing that I can do to bring peace in the world is to share "clear awareness of the world as it really is."

When we proclaim the nondual gospel of the Kingdom of God we are not irrelevant. We are not "so heavenly minded that we are of no earthly good" as they say. Just the opposite. Nonduality is deep peacemaking that political and military action can never accomplish. The realm of the Spirit is the front line of peacemaking. No political party or army will bring peace to earth until there is peace in the human heart.

Jesus was peacemaking when he refused to defend himself. He told his disciples to put away their weapons, saying "For those who take up the sword will die by the sword." If he were saying that today he would say, "Those who take up guns will perish by the gun." I like the translation, "Anyone who lives by fighting will die fighting." The nondual lifestyle is making peace by living peace.

Later in the Sermon on the Mount Jesus expounds on what nondual peacemaking looks like in action. He contrasts dualistic thinking with nondual action. He says, "You have heard that it was said, 'Eye for eye, and tooth for tooth.' But I tell you, do not resist an evil person. If anyone slaps you on the right cheek, turn to them the other cheek also. And if anyone wants to sue you and take your shirt, hand over your coat as well. If anyone forces you to go one mile, go with them two miles. Give to the one who asks you, and do not turn away from the one who wants to borrow from you. "You have heard that it was said, 'Love your neighbor and hate your enemy.' But I tell you, love your enemies and pray for those who persecute you, that you may be children of your Father in heaven."

In this section Jesus uses the phrase "children of God" just like when he says that peacemakers shall be called "children of God." In both places the Greek text literally says "sons of God." It is often translated "children of God" nowadays because that phrase is more inclusive of men and women. I understand the reason for inclusive language, but an inclusive translation here obscures the fact that Jesus uses the male form for a reason.

Jesus saw himself as the Son of God, and he is saying that others are too. That new identity was revealed in his baptismal experience. He did not see himself as the *only* Son of God or the *only begotten* Son of God. That distinction is a later development of Christianity. Jesus never made distinctions between himself and others. Just the opposite. By using the term "sons of God" in this beatitude Jesus is extending the term beyond himself to all who are peacemakers.

When we are making peace as Jesus made peace, then we are Children of God as Jesus is the Child of God. All who have seen our oneness with God, oneness with others, and oneness with creation - and who live and proclaim that oneness - are sons of God, children of God. That is the message of this beatitude. That is Christian nonduality. When that message is heard and heeded, then there is true peace.

Persecuted for Nonduality

The eighth and final beatitude in the Christ's Eightfold Path says, "Blessed are those who are persecuted because of righteousness, for theirs is the kingdom of heaven." It is immediately followed by what some consider to be a ninth beatitude, but is actually an expansion of the eighth. Jesus simply shifts from the third person to the second person. He says, "Blessed are you when people insult you, persecute you and falsely say all kinds of evil against you because of me. Rejoice and be glad, because great is your reward in heaven, for in the same way they persecuted the prophets who were before you." This coda is Jesus' way of bringing this set of nondual beatitudes to a conclusion and applying them directly to the reader.

The topic of this beatitude is persecution. I have never known persecution. Some evangelical Christians believe that Christians are being persecuted today in the United States. They aren't. They do not know what religious persecution is. Christianity is simply losing its place of privilege and power in the United States, and Christians think that is persecution. That is not persecution.

There is genuine religious persecution in the world, including persecution of Christians in some countries. Muslims are persecuted in some countries. The same with Jews and Buddhists, Hindus, Sikhs, Baha'is, Parsees and many other religious and ethnic minorities. Persecution tends to be most severe in nations where a fundamentalist form of religion or a militant form of atheism is in control of government. The lack of religious freedom is a serious problem in the world.

Yet Jesus is not talking about religious persecution in a general sense. He is speaking about being persecuted for giving voice to what is called nonduality. Jesus says, "Blessed are those who are persecuted because of righteousness." A more common translation is "for righteousness' sake." In an earlier chapter I explored what righteousness means. It means rightness, right relationship with reality, right perception of Reality.

Jesus is not using the word in the legalistic way that fundamentalists use it. He is not talking about having to set things right by means of a human sacrifice offered on an instrument of torture in order to appease an angry deity, so that God can impute God's righteousness to your divine balance sheet. That is a distortion that was developed later. Righteousness is a fundamental rightness in the universe that can be known here now. As Browning wrote: "God's in His heaven, All's right with the world!"

Knowing rightness by direct experience is what Jesus called entering the Kingdom of God or seeing the Kingdom of God. I call it unitive awareness or nondual awareness. One might call it Kingdom Consciousness or Christ consciousness. You could even call it righteousness consciousness. It is the awareness of cosmic rightness that is present here now.

In this beatitude Jesus says that declaring this nondual righteousness brings persecution upon the one who proclaims it. As I said, I have never known persecution. I have experienced what Jesus describes in the next sentence when he expands his definition of persecution to lesser forms of opposition. He says, "Blessed are you when people insult you, persecute you and falsely say all kinds of evil against you because of me."

I have had people insult me and falsely say all kinds of evil against me because I proclaim Jesus' message of nonduality. It has come almost exclusively from evangelical or fundamentalist Christians. It is ironic. Evangelicals tend to see themselves as the victims of a godless, secular, anti-Christian culture. They see themselves as being persecuted. But in my experience they are the ones doing the persecuting.

It is not hard to see how the Church has played the role of persecutors in Church history. The Inquisition, the Crusades, the pogroms, racism, anti-Semitism and the German Christian Movement of Nazi Germany come to mind. I see a resurgence of that mentality today, and it concerns me for the future of my country and American Christianity.

My experience of being insulted and spoken against has been mild. Nasty comments have been made online. Former evangelical friends have attacked me verbally. These insults and accusations are minor. They do not rise to the level of persecution. I have not been excommunicated like Meister Eckhart was – posthumously I might add – even though my message is basically the same as his. That is because I live in the 21st century and not the 14th.

In fact I have a good relationship with the American Baptist denomination, leaders and colleagues here in New Hampshire. That is because Baptists have historically been strong advocates for individual religious tolerance. At least in the north. That is changing rapidly among Southern Baptists, who are presently on a spree of excommunicating – they call it disfellowshipping – those who do not abide by their social, political and theological agenda.

I do not have to worry about that. I no longer have any relationship with the Southern Baptist Convention, even though I received two graduate degrees from a Southern Baptist seminary and have pastored Southern Baptist churches. Also I am retired. The community church I am part of in New Hampshire accepts me. They even invite me to preach occasionally!

Those in more conservative churches and denominations may have a different story. It depends on the church and denomination. People coming into unitive awareness ask me about this. They are concerned that they will be ostracized by their churches and their denominations if they start talking about this. I admit to them that this is possible. Jesus said that religious folks will treat us the way they treated him. Look what religious and political leaders did to Jesus! So it is a valid concern.

Yet what we get in return for speaking Truth is more than worth the price we pay. Jesus said, "Blessed are those who are persecuted because of righteousness, for theirs is the kingdom of heaven." So it is worth it. The Kingdom of Heaven is worth our earthy lives. As missionary Jim Eliot famously said, "He is no fool who gives what he cannot keep to gain what he cannot lose."

One of the best parts of this eighth beatitude is the final section. After blessing us for being persecuted, Jesus says, "Rejoice and be glad, because great is your reward in heaven, for in the same way they treated the prophets who were before you." Jesus compares us to prophets! What an honor!

The biblical prophets were almost always unpopular with the powers that be, both of the established religion of the land and the worldly leaders of the state. John the Baptist was imprisoned and beheaded. Jeremiah was imprisoned. Daniel was thrown in the lion's den and the fiery furnace. The Epistle to the Hebrews' "roll call of faith" describes how prophets were historically persecuted. Speaking truth to power always has a price.

Prophets spoke in the name of God. They spoke as God. That is important to remember when comparing nondual teaching with prophecy. Prophets said, "Thus saith the Lord." In other words they were speaking from God consciousness. The same with the psalmists. "Be still and know that I am God" says the psalmist. The prophets and psalmists knew God consciousness. They were speaking as Nondual Awareness or Divine Consciousness, although they did not call it that.

Divine consciousness is not just for saints of long ago whose writings got published in the Bible. It is for us today. On Pentecost the Holy Spirit filled the early Christians, and they spoke under the influence of God. Peter explained it to the crowd saying that this was the fulfillment of the prophecy of Joel, saying, "In the last days, God says, I will pour out my Spirit on all people. Your sons and daughters will prophesy, your young men will see visions, your old men will dream dreams. Even on my servants, both men and women, I will pour out my Spirit in those days, and they will prophesy."

Unitive awareness is a shift in perspective from the human to the divine. It is seeing and speaking not as individual selves, but as the Divine Self. It is speaking in the prophetic voice. It is speaking from Nondual Awareness. Jesus spoke as the Son of God, calling God his Father and saying he was one with God. That is why he was persecuted.

He warned us that if we speak like he did, we should not be surprised if people treat us as they treated him. "'A servant is not greater than his master.' If they persecuted me, they will persecute you also." He said, "A disciple is not above his teacher, nor a servant above his master. It is enough for a disciple to be like his teacher, and a servant like his master. If the head of the house has been called Beelzebul, how much more the members of his household!" Therefore we are to expect opposition to this nondual message. We have been warned by Jesus. We have also been blessed by Jesus in this beatitude and all the beatitudes. What more could we want?

Who Does Jesus Say You Are?

In Christianity there is a lot of talk about who Jesus is. Jesus himself encouraged this line of questioning, saying to his disciples: "Who do people say that I am?" He received a lot of answers, including Peter's famous profession, "You are the Christ, the Son of God!" When on trial Jesus was repeatedly asked who he was. He was executed for what he and others were saying about him.

The Gospel of John is famous for its seven "I am" statements in which Jesus identifies himself using seven symbols and metaphors. "I am the Bread of Life. I am the Light of the world. I am the Way, the Truth and the Life" and so forth. They are all based on the famous "I am" statement in the story of the burning bush in Exodus, where God says "I am that I am."

There are also "You are" statements made by Jesus, telling us what we are. In looking through the Bible I have found three statements that Jesus made about who we are. The first two are in the early verses of the Sermon on the Mount, immediately after the beatitudes. The first teaching is "You are the salt of the earth." His full statement is: "You are the salt of the earth, but if salt has lost its taste, how shall its saltiness be restored? It is no longer good for anything except to be thrown out and trampled under people's feet."

Jesus says we are salt. There have been a lot of sermons preached on those words. Most of them read later Church theology back into Jesus' words. Preachers wax eloquent about the medicinal, purifying and preservative characteristics of salt. Jesus focuses solely on the taste of salt.

When we put salt in food or water we can't see it, but we can taste it. Jesus is saying that our true nature is like that – invisible yet undeniably present. A passage in the Chandogya Upanishad uses the same metaphor. A father is giving spiritual instruction to his son. The boy asks his father to teach him about the Self. The father says:

> *"Place this salt in water and bring it here tomorrow morning." The boy did. "Where is that salt?" his father asked. "I do not see it." "Sip here. How does it taste?" "Salty, Father." "And here? And there?" "I taste salt everywhere." "It is everywhere, though we see it not." "Just so, dear one, the Self is everywhere, within all things, although we see him not. There is nothing that does not come from him. Of everything he is the inmost essence. He is the truth; he is the Self supreme. You are that, Shvetaketu; you are that."*

Jesus teaches the same truth. We are the salt of the earth. We are the essence present in all the earth. This essence cannot be seen but it is real. Jesus then gives a paradoxical statement about salt losing its taste: *"If salt has lost its taste, how shall its saltiness be restored? It is no longer good for anything except to be thrown out and trampled under people's feet."* This of course cannot happen. Salt cannot not become unsalty. If it is unsalty, it is not salt. We cannot be other than what we are. This is the wonderful thing about discovering our true nature. There is nothing we have to do to be who we are. All we have to do is be, which is effortless.

The only way salt can be tasteless is if we mistake something for salt that is not salt, like mistaking a grain of sand for salt. If we make this mistake, we will break a tooth. It causes suffering. Likewise when we mistake ourselves for something we are not, it causes suffering. We mistake the body for who we are. We mistake our possessions, occupation, reputation, mind, thoughts, feelings, or personality for who we are. We think we are what we are not. That is the problem. We are the salt of the earth, the essence of earthly existence. That essence is what we are. Be who you are.

The second metaphor Jesus uses is light. He says, "You are the light of the world." Here are his full words: *"You are the light of the world. A city set on a hill cannot be hidden. Nor do people light a lamp and put it under a basket, but on a stand, and it gives light to all in the house. In the same way, let your light shine before others, so that they may see your good works and give glory to your Father who is in heaven."*

This is a powerful metaphor. What is light? Scientists do not know. Light is a mystery. It is energy that behaves like both a particle and a wave. It is literally timeless. If we were to travel at the speed of light time would stop. We are the light of the world. The word for world used by Jesus is cosmos. We are the light of the cosmos, the universe. We are a mystery that cannot be understood. We are timeless. Time is an invention of our minds, but we are not bound by it.

The Bible says God is light. The first epistle of John says, "This is the message we have heard from Him [meaning Jesus] and announce to you, that God is Light, and in Him there is no darkness at all." God is light and we are light, according to Jesus.

Like with the metaphor of salt, Jesus focuses on one aspect of light. It shines. You cannot see light, yet everything is seen by it. When you are walking outside you do not notice light but notice everything by the light. That is what we are. It is like awareness or consciousness, depending which word you want to use. You cannot see it, but you see by it.

This awareness is not secret knowledge available only to a religious or spiritual elite. It is a city set on a hill, obvious to all who have eyes to see. When he said this Jesus probably had in mind the city of Sepphoris, which was the provincial capital located not far from Nazareth. As a construction worker, Jesus was probably one of the workers who rebuilt it. A city set on a hill cannot be hidden. Who and what we are is not hidden. It is absolutely obvious. It is just a matter of opening our eyes.

You are the light of the world. This "You are" statement has a parallel in one of Jesus' "I AM" statements. He says, "I am the light of the world. Whoever follows me will not walk in darkness, but will have the light of life." This verse occurs in the Gospel of John shortly before Jesus said: "Before Abraham was, I am," referring to the words of God at the Burning Bush, which shone with the light of "I AM." Jesus had this self-identity – this experience - of being the light of the world, and he said we are also the light of the world. Be who you are. Do not cover it up this light with some other identity, a false self. Be who you are.

The third "You are" statement spoken by Jesus is not found in the Sermon on the Mount, but I will include it here because it echoes the Sermon's teaching. It is found in the Gospel of John. Jesus says, "I am the vine; you are the branches. Whoever abides in me and I in him, he it is that bears much fruit, for apart from me you can do nothing. If anyone does not abide in me he is thrown away like a branch and withers; and the branches are gathered, thrown into the fire, and burned."

You are branches, and therefore you are part of the vine that Jesus identifies as his nature. He is talking about grape vines, of course. For a decade I had grapevines on the property of a parsonage, where I lived in as a pastor. At that time I learned a little about tending a vineyard. Not very much, but I learned a little. I tried my hand at pruning the branches to produce stronger grapes.

I found out quickly that it is difficult to tell where the vine stops and the branches begin.

There is no clear difference between the trunk, cordon, arms, and shoots except age. The difference is a matter of semantics. We label parts with different words, and then think they are different. They are not. They are all grapevine. That is the point of Jesus' metaphor. The vine and the branches are one. When they are separated, they are worthless and do not produce fruit. When they abide in each other, they are fruitful.

That is the common theme of these three 'You are' statements of Jesus. They are about abiding in Oneness. The salt is one with the water or food. The light is one with the space and all objects illuminated by the light. The branches are one with the vine. We are one with Christ. That oneness is what we are. Thinking we are separate is like salt that is tasteless, a lamp hidden under a basket, or a branch without a vine. When we abide in the vine, the fruit of unitive awareness happens. We experience oneness with the One we call God. That is who we are. Be who you are.

A Nondual Approach to Scripture

After Jesus talks about our spiritual identity, he gives his approach to scripture. Scripture is important to Christians. The historic confessions of faith in my tradition as well as other Protestant traditions normally begin with a section on the inspiration and authority of scripture, which serves as a foundation for everything else. Therefore it is not surprising that Jesus does the same thing in his Sermon on the Mount.

> *Do not think that I have come to abolish the Law or the Prophets; I have not come to abolish them but to fulfill them. For truly I tell you, until heaven and earth disappear, not the smallest letter, not the least stroke of a pen, will by any means disappear from the Law until everything is accomplished. Therefore anyone who sets aside one of the least of these commands and teaches others accordingly will be called least in the kingdom of heaven, but whoever practices and teaches these commands will be called great in the kingdom of heaven. For I tell you that unless your righteousness surpasses that of the Pharisees and the teachers of the law, you will certainly not enter the kingdom of heaven.*

Jesus is defending himself against the accusations being made against him that he was abolishing the Scriptures, which he calls the Law and the Prophets. The Law was also known

63

as the Torah. The Torah and the Prophets were the two parts of Jewish Scriptures at that time. The third section, the Writings, had not yet been canonized.

Jesus' most frequent critics were the Pharisees, who accused him of breaking the Law because he worked on the Sabbath. The Sabbath was one of God's top ten rules, and they accused Jesus of being a Sabbath breaker. They also accused him of breaking the ritual purity laws of the Torah by not washing his hands and by associating with people who were unclean according to the Law.

So the primary accusation against Jesus by the religious people of his time was that he was abolishing the Torah, the first five books of the Bible and the heart of Hebrew Scripture. The Sadducees, who were the religious conservatives of the day, considered the Torah to be the only Scriptures. They did not accept the Prophets. In other words they were accusing Jesus of throwing out the Bible, not accepting the authority the Scriptures.

That is the accusation most often lobbed against me, so I feel like I am in good company! Jesus refutes that accusation, saying, "I did not come to abolish the Scriptures, but to fulfill them!" This is Jesus' nondual approach to Scripture. Nondual teachings do not abolish the scriptures; they fulfil them. Jesus loved the Hebrew Scriptures. He read them, studied them and quoted them. We can determine his favorite books by which ones he quotes most often. He particularly loved the Psalms, Deuteronomy and Isaiah.

You can tell by his words here that Jesus held a high view of scripture. Yet he did not have the fundamentalist view of scripture that Christian evangelicals adhere to today. Jesus never used words like inerrant or infallible to describe the Bible. He was not a legalist concerning Scripture the way the Pharisees were. He had a much more open and creative approach to Scripture.

Jesus was not a fundamentalist, but he did not throw out the scriptures of his religion either. Just the opposite. He said, "For truly I tell you, until heaven and earth disappear, not the smallest letter, not the least stroke of a pen, will by any means disappear from the Law until everything is accomplished." In other words he wanted to keep scriptures intact. But only "until everything is accomplished."

The apostle Paul had a similar approach to scripture. In his letter to the Galatians the apostle Paul likens the Law to a schoolmaster. He writes: "Before faith came, we were kept under the Law, shut up unto the faith which should afterwards be revealed. The Law was our schoolmaster to bring us unto Christ... But after that faith is come, we are no longer under a schoolmaster. For you are all children of God by faith in Christ Jesus."

Other translations use terms other than schoolmaster to describe the role of scripture, words like guardian, trainer, tutor, guide or disciplinarian. Scriptures are meant to train us until they have fulfilled their purpose. In other words Scriptures are useful, which is exactly the word used in the most famous statement about Scripture in the Bible. "All Scripture is inspired by God and useful for teaching, for reproof, for correction, and for training in righteousness." (2 Timothy 3:16)

It is similar to an analogy that the Buddha used. He told the story about a man traveling along a path and coming to a river. He wanted to cross it, but found no boat or bridge. So he built a simple raft. Laying on the raft to keep himself afloat, the man paddled with his hands and feet and reached the safety of the other shore. Then he could continue his journey on land. What should the man do with his raft? Should he carry it with him or leave it behind? He would leave it of course, the Buddha said. The Buddha explained that the dharma (his teaching) is like a raft. It is useful, but after it has fulfilled its purpose you do not carry it with you. Yet it can be preserved for others who would want to cross.

Scripture was like that for Jesus. It is useful "until everything is accomplished." Another phrase Jesus uses is that it is useful "until heaven and earth disappear." That is usually interpreted to mean the Scriptures will remain to the end of the world, which is a valid interpretation. It can also mean the disappearance of the duality of heaven and earth, which happens at spiritual awakening. Heaven and earth disappear, and all is seen as one. Jesus had both senses – historic and eternal - in mind. He understood that there would come a time when nondual Reality, the

Kingdom of God, is fully manifested for all to see.

One could also say that studying the Scriptures provides the basics. It is like practicing scales when you are learning to play an instrument. It is like learning the essentials of form, perspective and color when learning to paint. Or learning the basics in dance or any art form. In any field you have to learn the basics first. You study and obey the rules. Later you bend the rules in creative ways, which is what Jesus did with the Sabbath laws and ritual purity rules. Jesus does not abolish the rules. He does not reject the basics. He affirms them, yet goes beyond them.

He realizes they are necessary in the spiritual life. Jesus says, "Therefore anyone who sets aside one of the least of these commands and teaches others accordingly will be called least in the kingdom of heaven, but whoever practices and teaches these commands will be called great in the kingdom of heaven." Then he points us beyond the basics. He goes on to say: "For I tell you that unless your righteousness surpasses that of the Pharisees and the teachers of the law, you will certainly not enter the Kingdom of Heaven."

Jesus is saying that you have to surpass the basics to enter the Kingdom of Heaven. That is what Jesus' opponents did not understand. The Pharisees and teachers of the Torah were good at following religious laws, but Jesus said they were not entering the Kingdom of Heaven. Fundamentalists today are good at following the religious rules of Scripture, but they are not entering the Kingdom of God. Moses, who was the Lawgiver, did not enter the Promised Land. He only saw it from afar. To enter the Kingdom of God you have to go beyond Scriptures to where the Scriptures point. Scriptures are pointers, not the destination. They are words, not the Reality to which the words point.

In the rest of this section of the Sermon on the Mount, Jesus points beyond Scripture and the traditional interpretation of Scripture. The next few teachings of Jesus contain the same words. Jesus says, "You have heard that it was said ... but I say to you." He begins, "You have heard that it was said" and then he quotes a commandment of Scripture. Then he supersedes the commandment with his own teaching, saying, "But I say to you."

Jesus' teachings go beyond Scripture. That is why he was opposed by the religious authorities and crucified. He was not rejecting Scripture as the religious leaders thought he was; he was fulfilling them. In the next chapter I will explore five teachings that Jesus gives as example of how nonduality fulfills the teachings of Scripture.

The Nondual Ethics of Jesus

Nonduality underlies the ethics of Jesus. His ethical teachings in the Sermon on the Mount have a pattern. First Jesus says, "You have heard that it was said..." and then he quotes a passage from the Torah. Then he adds, "but I say to you." Then he proceeds to give his teaching. In other words he says, "The Bible says this ... but I say this." He was not negating what the Bible said. He was building upon it and completing it. He was fulfilling it.

I am going to take each of his sayings in this section of the Sermon on the Mount and see how his teachings reflect a nondual ethic that goes beyond dualistic understandings of right and wrong, us and them. Living from nonduality is entirely different than living by moral rules and laws. When one is aware of the one Reality that unites everything, one lives naturally out of our nondual nature rather than trying to figure out with our heads what we should do. Paul calls this "walking in the Spirit" as opposed to obeying the Law.

The first commandment, which Jesus addresses, is the commandment against murder. "You have heard that it was said to the people long ago, 'You shall not murder, and anyone who murders will be subject to judgment.' But I tell you that anyone who is angry with a brother or sister will be subject to judgment."

Laws against killing people are important for order in society. They are necessary, and not to be abolished. But they are of limited value when it comes to mature spirituality. It takes little effort for most of us to refrain from murdering people. So Jesus takes this to a deeper level. He leads us into self-inquiry. He guides us to examine where the urge to murder comes from. He identifies it as anger.

Where does anger come from? It comes from ego. Ego is protecting itself. One way it does that is with anger. We feel threatened in some way, and we immediately respond to protect ourselves – our self. We may do this with violence, but we also do it with angry words. So Jesus says, "anyone who says to a brother or sister, 'Raca,' is answerable to the court."

Raca is an Aramaic insult. Imagine the nastiest words that a person might call someone they are angry with. Those words are the modern equivalent of Raca. Then Jesus goes on, "And anyone who says, 'You fool!' will be in danger of the fire of hell." Insults come from somewhere, and he is calling our attention to where. They come from fear. We are afraid at a deep level, and so we lash out.

Jesus mentions judgment and hell. From a nondual perspective he is not talking about an apocalyptic event sometime in the future. There is only here and now. In talking about judgment he is talking about the experience of guilt here and now. Hell is what we make of our lives here and now, when we are consumed by anger. Anger is an inner hellfire that burns within us. It sometimes boils over into hateful words or violence that creates hell for others. Jesus leads us into self-inquiry to address that inner guilt, suffering and fear. The source of these emotions is the ego. When the ego is seen through, then anger, hate and violence dissipate.

The second issue, which Jesus deals with, is adultery. This is another one of God's Top Ten. Jesus said, "You have heard that it was said, 'You shall not commit adultery.' But I tell you that anyone who looks at a woman lustfully has already committed adultery with her in his heart."

Jesus again encourages self-inquiry. He goes beyond the physical act of adultery to the source of adultery, which he identifies as lust. Lust originates in the body. To make that point Jesus uses the argument of *reductio ad absurdum*. He suggests that people could cut off the offending parts of the body, whether the eye or hand of some other part. Some people have actually taken Jesus literally! Origen reportedly castrated himself! It is obvious that we are not supposed to take Jesus literally! If you start cutting off offending body parts, you won't have any a body left! Jesus' teaching technique is to get people to think in new ways by suggesting the preposterous alternatives.

Investigate lust and you see that all emotions and physical sensations are simply energy in the body. A little bit of meditation reveals that quite quickly. Sensations in the body ebb and flow. We don't need to act on them. Let them come and go. Watch them as they come and go like

71

clouds blowing across the sky. We do not have to act on these thoughts and urges. We are not these bodily urges. We are the space that these physical and mental energies flow through. See that for yourself. Act from that space and not the energy flowing through that space. That is nondual ethics.

Jesus follows up his teaching on adultery by relating it to divorce, using the same approach. This is a section loved by misogynists and legalists, who entirely miss the point. Jesus invites us to look deeper than law. He says, "It was also said, 'Whoever divorces his wife, let him give her a certificate of divorce.' But I say to you that everyone who divorces his wife, except on the ground of sexual immorality, makes her commit adultery, and whoever marries a divorced woman commits adultery."

Jesus is inviting men to do self-inquiry concerning why they divorce their wives. The Law permitted only men to divorce. And men could divorce their wives for any reason. That freedom was abused. Divorced women found themselves vulnerable to poverty and homelessness in a male-dominated culture. Men used the Law to sin against their wives!

Jesus undercuts this egotism by saying that a man could only divorce his wife if she had already broken the marriage covenant by committing adultery. That eliminated ninety-nine percent of all divorces in that culture. Jesus was protecting women. But legalistic Christians today turn Jesus' words into a new law that puts a stigma on divorce and remarriage, which the Scriptures never intended. Jesus is not giving a new law, which could lead to a new legalism. He was inviting us beyond Scripture to self-inquiry in regard to divorce.

Then he addresses oaths. "Again, you have heard that it was said to the people long ago, 'Do not break your oath, but fulfill to the Lord the vows you have made.' But I tell you, do not swear an oath at all.... All you need to say is simply 'Yes' or 'No'; anything beyond this comes from the evil one." Jesus is talking about keeping the promises we make.

When we do self-inquiry into the promise-keeping process, it leads quickly to the issue of who exactly is making the promises? We see it is the ego. It is the individual personal self, which likes to think of itself as in control of everything. If it were really in control, it wouldn't need to make oaths and promises in the first place. That is what Jesus is getting at. He says, "Just say yes or no, and leave it at that. Anything more is from the evil one." The evil one is a symbol for the ego.

The next ethical issue Jesus addresses has application to all sorts of situations. He says, "You have heard that it was said, 'Eye for eye, and tooth for tooth.' But I tell you, do not resist an evil person. If anyone slaps you on the right cheek, turn to them the other cheek also." He follows it up in a few verses with this: "You have heard that it was said, 'Love your neighbor and hate your enemy.' But I tell you, love your enemies and pray for those who persecute you, that you may be children of your Father in heaven."

In these sentences Jesus comes to the heart of how identity determines ethics. He says "Do not resist an evil person," which we just identified as the ego. He is telling us not only how to relate to other people but how to relate to our ego. If you fight it, it only grows stronger. The solution is nonresistance. When the ego has nothing to fight against, it dies.

That is how we relate to others egos as well. Egos are the problem in the spiritual life and in relationships. If we view people as enemy egos that are a threat to our ego, we will act accordingly. If we see everyone as essentially one, there I no other to fear. Then we love others as ourselves because we see they are ourselves. They are us. As I have often said, there is only one Self in the universe. That Self is incarnated in every person we meet – friend and foe. Look into the eyes of another person and you will recognize the same self looking back. Loving others – even our enemies – is loving our Self from the Self, the True Self.

The ego, on the other hand, always defends itself. That is its nature. That is what Jesus' statement about being slapped on the cheek is about. The ego justifies self-defense by making people into enemies. Likewise the body defends itself naturally. That is built into the body by evolution; it is the instinct to survive. That is why the law allows for self-defense. Jesus is going beyond the Law and beyond the natural reaction of the ego and the body.

Nonduality reveals that we are not the body or the ego. For that reason nondual ethics goes beyond protecting ego and body. That is what the Cross represents. This cruciform approach is radical in ethics. It means we are free from obeying body-mind instincts. That opens up all sorts of other possibilities. Most importantly it opens the way for our true nature, which is unconditional love, to operate through these body-minds. This leads to living nonviolence in all areas of life. The True nature, the Spirit, can then guide us.

When we live from nondual awareness, moral actions come spontaneously and naturally. We are whole, complete. That is why Jesus ends this section with the words "Be perfect, therefore, as your heavenly Father is perfect." The Greek word translated perfect means whole, complete, mature, or fulfilled. Jesus is saying: Be whole. Be one with God. Then Oneness directs our ethical choices. That is nondual ethics.

Nondual Spiritual Practices

People ask me what spiritual practices I recommend to help them open up to the realization of what Jesus calls the Kingdom of God. I tell them that as far as I know there are no such practices. I was not practicing any spiritual practices at the time. In fact I had rejected all religious and spiritual practices. Therefore when this spiritual shift happened, I attributed it purely to grace.

Having said that, I have to admit that for decades previously I had engaged in spiritual practices. I practiced forms of contemplative prayer and meditation for many years. I had also done the traditional Christian disciplines of verbal prayer and Scripture study. I read spiritual books, especially devotional classics. I have been involved in Christian worship all my adult life. Therefore one could make a case that those practices prepared the ground for spiritual awakening to sprout. Yet it feels like pure grace.

In any case Jesus recommends some spiritual practices in the Sermon on the Mount. Like everything else he said, these practices were rooted in Kingdom Consciousness or Nondual Awareness. Jesus does not present these spiritual disciplines in the form of commands. He did not tell his followers that they had to do spiritual exercises. Instead he assumed that his followers would do such practices, and he told them how to do them.

Jesus starts off this section with the following words, which serve as the theme of the whole section. "Be careful not to practice your righteousness in front of others to be seen by them. If you do, you will have no reward from your Father in heaven." Jesus is warning against doing spiritual practices for the wrong reasons. Specifically he was warning against the ego using spiritual practices for its own reasons. He regularly criticized the Pharisees and Sadducees for their displays of religiosity. He called them hypocrites for doing this.

That is certainly a danger in every spiritual tradition. The ego coopts everything for its own purpose, including spirituality. In so doing it undermines spiritual practices. For that reason Jesus' advice concerning spiritual practices is "be careful." It is not about what spiritual practice is best. It is about why you are doing it, and more importantly who is doing it. If the ego is doing it for egoic purposes, the practice will not go beyond the ego.

Once again – just like in the last section – Jesus leads us into self-inquiry. People of all religions are vulnerable to displays of ego masquerading as righteousness. To guard against this problem Jesus' advice is to do everything as privately as possible. We can't start making rules about this or we will fall into legalism, which is another egoic trap. Instead we simply need to be careful that our spiritual practices are originating from a divine source and not an egoic source.

The first practice Jesus mentions is almsgiving. This is called charitable giving today. In an earlier age it was called charity. The word charity has bad connotations now, but it comes from the Latin word for love. If Christians practiced giving alms today in the United States, there would have no poverty in our country. Many Americans complain about taxes going to social programs, but if Christians did what Jesus told us to do, there would be no need for these programs.

Jesus defines almsgiving as giving to the needy. "So when you give to the needy..." he says. He assumes we will give to the needy. Unfortunately this type of giving has been replaced in Christianity by giving to the church. Christians are encouraged to contribute generously to the church coffers.

Many Christians tithe their income and hope that it will get to those in need. In reality most of it doesn't. Buildings, salaries and employee benefits make up almost all of the church's budget. It is lucky of a tenth of a church's budget goes to "missions." Even most of the missions go to salaries and buildings of missions organizations. Church has turned into a business. In megachurches, it has become big business with pastors drawing huge salaries and perks. Only a tiny fraction of the money that Christians give to the church goes to people in need. If churches gave all the money they collected to what Jesus calls almsgiving, it would wipe out homelessness and hunger.

I have nothing against giving money to churches. I made my living as a local church pastor for forty years, so it would be hypocritical for me to knock it now that I am retired. I give money to my local church. Jesus didn't oppose giving money to the temple. Jesus praised the poor widow who put her "widow's mite" into the temple treasury. But this is not the almsgiving that Jesus is talking about in the Sermon on the Mount. Giving to the church does not take the place of giving to those in need.

Why give to the needy? The answer is found in nonduality. We give to the needy because we are one with the needy. They are us. That is the meaning of compassion. It means to "suffer with." Jesus said, "As you did it to the least of these my brothers and sisters, you have done it to me." He considered himself indistinguishable from his brothers and sisters. So are we. As I repeatedly say, we love our neighbors as ourselves because they are ourselves.

That unitive reality determines how we give. Jesus goes on, "So when you give to the needy, [not *if* but *when*] do not announce it with trumpets, as the hypocrites do in the synagogues and on the streets, to be honored by others. Truly I tell you, they have received their reward in full. But when you give to the needy, do not let your left hand know what your right hand is doing, so that your giving may be in secret."

Jesus is telling us to give unselfconsciously. Jesus is referring to the type of gift that is so selfless that we are hardly aware that we are giving it. It comes naturally. This is Kingdom giving, which comes from Kingdom consciousness – nondual awareness. The ego, on the other hand, does what is best for itself. If it gives money, it wants something in return. It wants to be acknowledged by people. At the very least it wants a tax deduction.

Jesus says that spiritual practices are to flow from the Divine Self, not the egoic self. To use Christian language, it flows from the Spirit and not the flesh. In Christian terminology flesh is simply another word for ego. When we give, let it be God giving through us with as little interference from the self as possible.

The next spiritual discipline Jesus recommends is prayer. "And when you pray, do not be like the hypocrites, for they love to pray standing in the synagogues and on the street corners to be seen by others. Truly I tell you, they have received their reward in full. But when you pray, go into your room, close the door and pray to your Father, who is unseen. Then your Father, who sees what is done in secret, will reward you."

He doesn't tell us *how* to pray. He will get to that in a minute. First he tells us *where* to pray: in private. The ego loves an audience. The Self – the True Self, the Spiritual Self – knows there is no audience. All is One, and that One is God. There is no other, so it is foolish to put on a show for others. Pray without ego.

Then he tells us *how* to pray, or rather how *not* to pray. "And when you pray, do not keep on babbling like pagans, for they think they will be heard because of their many words. Do not be like them, for your Father knows what you need before you ask him."

In other words, use a minimum of words. His example of brevity is the Lord's Prayer. I will devote the next chapter exclusively to this famous prayer. For now I will simply say that the point of the Lord's Prayer is brevity. He didn't expect this prayer to be memorized and repeated as a ritual by his followers. That is not Jesus' style.

Prayer without words is even better. I seldom use words during prayer. They get in the way. They are clumsy and inaccurate. Jesus says God knows what we need before we ask, so what is the point of voicing them? Words are for communication, and communication implies duality. Words put a distance between God and us. That is the opposite of oneness!

Words are tools of the personal self. Using words in prayer is fine as far as it goes. I would never discourage verbal prayer. If the ego needs to speak to God, let it speak. If you need to speak to God in prayer, speak. But keep it brief. I would rather simply be present in the Divine Presence without dualistic words or thoughts or prayers or practices. I resonate with the words of the apostle Paul in his Letter to the Romans. He says, "Likewise the Spirit helps us in our weakness, for we do not know how to pray as we ought, but that very Spirit intercedes with groanings too deep for words." Prayer is deeper than words. It is simply abiding in God. That is nondual prayer.

The Lord's Prayer – Nondual Style

As I mentioned in the last chapter, Jesus offered the Lord's Prayer as an example of brevity in prayer. It is not the greatest prayer that Jesus ever offered in the gospels. In my opinion that honor would go to his Gethsemane prayer recorded in the 17th chapter of John's gospel. That is the longest prayer of Jesus and explicitly nondual. In the Gethsemane prayer Jesus prays that we might know oneness with God as he knows it.

The Lord' Prayer, on the other hand, is not explicitly nondual. At first reading it looks very dualistic. Jesus addresses his Father in heaven, implying a distance between him and God. He prays for the Father's Kingdom to come, as if it were not already present. He asks for forgiveness from God, which presupposes that he is separated from God by sin. By the way, Jesus' request for forgiveness is a stumbling block for traditional Christians who consider Jesus sinless!

Traditional interpretations of the Lord's Prayer find a way around this Christological problem, by saying that Jesus was not really asking forgiveness for himself. They say that Jesus was modeling a prayer for his sinful disciples, not for his sinless self. That seems disingenuous to me. Nowhere does Jesus say or imply that he is sinless. At the end of the prayer Jesus mentions the evil one, which is the epitome of dualism.

So there appears to be a lot of dualism in the Lord's Prayer, unlike the nondualism of the Gethsemane Prayer. Why this difference? For one thing, in Gethsemane he is praying privately at the end of his ministry. In the Lord's Prayer he is teaching publicly at the beginning of his ministry. Like all preachers, he knew that you preach to people where they are.

I learned this firsthand after this nondual shift in awareness eleven years ago. At first I said nothing to anyone because I did not have the words. When I found some words to describe the indescribable weeks later, I tried to communicate nondual awareness in sermons. I got a lot of blank stares from my congregation.

After a few weeks of doing this, I learned to present this message in smaller doses. I peppered my sermons with stories and metaphors that pointed to nonduality. I found that it worked better. Jesus did the same thing in his public teaching. The gospels say that Jesus would teach the crowds in parables and then explain them privately to his disciples later.

When I preach from the pulpit these days, I speak differently than I do in my podcast or YouTube channel. I use different language. In sermons I use traditional Christian language and show how it points beyond itself to the oneness of God and our oneness with God. That is what Jesus is doing in the Lord's Prayer. The Lord's Prayer uses dualistic language to point to nondual reality.

Let's interpret the text. Jesus begins the prayer addressing "our Father in heaven." That sounds as if he were separate from God, as if God is way off in the sky somewhere. We need to interpret this in light of Jesus' statement "I and the Father are one." He does not mean simply one in purpose, the way some interpreters say. Elsewhere he clearly says, "The words I say to you are not just my own. Rather, it is the Father, living in me, who is doing his work. Believe me when I say that I am in the Father and the Father is in me...." In John's gospel Jesus is clearly communicating a nondual understanding of himself and the Father.

Matthew's gospel is more dualistic. Yet even here Jesus is trying to bring God closer by the use of the term Father, rather than more common terms for God. To address God as Father was revolutionary in his time. The term is seldom used for God in the Old Testament. Elsewhere Jesus uses the word Abba, which is an even more intimate term for God.

Also "heavenly" does not mean way off in space somewhere. It means spiritual, not a physical place up in the sky beyond the clouds. Heaven is the spiritual dimension here and now. Jesus says that the Kingdom of Heaven is within us. That is how close God is. Closer than our jugular vein, the Quran says. Jesus is addressing a spiritual God, which he feels intimately one with – the Father in him and him in the Father. That is nonduality. Jesus uses the dualistic language of "heavenly Father" to point to nondual reality.

Then he says, "Hallowed be thy name." The word "hallowed" means holy or sacred. Those who interpret this word in a dualistic fashion stress the separation between holy and unholy, sacred and profane, clean and unclean, God and human. There is another way to look at "holy." The English word holy comes from the Greek word holos which means whole or one. We get the word holistic from it.

Yet the Greek word used in the Lord's Prayer is hagios, which means to purify or cleanse. One could interpret this dualistically to mean to purify from evil, uncleanness and the profane. That is the approach of the Pharisees. They separated themselves from people they considered unclean, sinful or evil. That is the dualistic approach. Jesus did not do that.

One can also interpret this word in a nondual manner. Hagios is not what separates us from God but what unites us to God. For example hagios is the apostle Paul's favorite term for followers of Jesus. We are hagios, usually translated saints. This does not mean we are spiritual superheroes. It means we are one with the holy God. Knowing that union purifies us, sanctifies us. Our sight is purified. We see as God sees. In spiritual awakening what appeared to be many is seen as one whole. Two becomes one.

That is also the theme of the next line. Jesus says, "thy kingdom come, thy will be done, on earth as it is in heaven." This is explicitly talking about heaven and earth becoming one. We see this vision also in the Book of Revelation, where the heaven and earth are united. Looking at this dualistically, this is the Kingdom of God coming to earth. Yet if the Kingdom of God is already here, as Jesus said, then the Kingdom has already come.

As Revelation says, "The kingdoms of this world are become the kingdom of our Lord." It is simply a matter of seeing this reality now. When one sees this, then one sees that everything that happens is God's will. God's will is done on earth as it is in heaven *now*! That is the nondual perspective. That changes how we pray. When all of humanity sees this, a shift of cosmic proportion occurs. Then the Kingdom of God is realized in history, although actually that has always been the case spiritually.

In the meantime – until everyone sees the Kingdom of God - we carry on as usual, eating our daily bread. "Give us this day our daily bread." This is Jesus' version of the Zen saying, "Chop wood, carry water." Whether one sees the Kingdom of God here and now, or expect it to come some day in the future, we still need to eat.

Jesus' phrase "daily bread" is a reference to the manna in the wilderness in the Hebrew Scriptures. God provided the Hebrews with miraculous bread from heaven for forty years as they were wandering in the wilderness. Every morning the Hebrews went out and gathered manna from heaven. The key element of the story is that they had to pick it *every day*. It was daily bread. If they tried to store manna till the next day, it would spoil. Daily bread points to living here and now, and not in some imagined future.

Now we come to the verses about forgiving our debts - or trespasses or sins, depending on the gospel and the translation. That also seems to presuppose duality until we realize what forgiveness is. Forgiveness reunites those who have become separated. It breaks down barriers. Enemies reconcile. It brings together. It makes two one. It unites God and humanity. Jesus says nothing about the need for sacrifices on an altar or a cross as a prerequisite for divine forgiveness. That was not Jesus' gospel. That was later Christianity's gospel. Jesus says that our forgiveness is dependent on us forgiving.

He prays, "And forgive us our debts, as we forgive our debtors." Jesus goes on to explicitly say: "For if you forgive other people when they sin against you, your heavenly Father will also forgive you. But if you do not forgive others their sins, your Father will not forgive your sins." That addendum is conveniently omitted from the Church's recitation of the Lord's Prayer. This means that if we live oneness with others, there is oneness with God. Forgiveness all the way around. You can't get any more nondual than that.

Finally Jesus mentions the evil one. "And lead us not into temptation, but deliver us from evil" or more accurately "from the evil one." Christians struggle with the suggestion that God could ever lead us into temptation. The pope even changed the wording of the prayer recently. Instead of "lead us not into temptation," it now reads, "do not let us fall into temptation." I understand the motivation for the change, but it is misguided. It undercuts the point I just made earlier, which is that God's will is being done now on earth in all things, for those with eyes to see.

Lastly I have talked about evil and the evil one, the devil or Satan, in other places, so I will not repeat myself here. I will just say that the devil is a product of dualistic thinking. So is evil. Evil is done by those enslaved to duality. There is a greater wholeness that includes what we label as good and evil. Spiritual awakening is seeing what we might call this Greater Good, the Tao, the Holistic One that supersedes and includes all duality of good and evil. The whole is seen as the Divine at work. God's will is done on earth as in heaven.

Fasting from Self

Both fasting and voluntary poverty are disciplines that are well-known in Christian monastic traditions, as well as in other spiritual traditions. Like the previous disciplines that Jesus mentions in the Sermon on the Mount, he does not instruct his followers to engage in the practice of fasting. In fact he and his disciples were criticized for *not* fasting.

A few chapters after the Sermon on the Mount in the Gospel of Matthew, we find the disciples of John the Baptist challenging Jesus on this issue. "Then the disciples of John came to him, saying, 'Why do we and the Pharisees fast, but your disciples do not fast?'" The Jesus movement was known for *not* fasting. The only time the gospels mention Jesus fasting was during the forty days following his baptism, before he began his public ministry.

A few chapters later Jesus sums up religious leaders' attitude toward him when it came to fasting. He said that they were calling him "a glutton and drunkard, a friend of tax collectors and sinners!" It is clear that Jesus and his followers were not known for fasting.

Yet Jesus says in the Sermon on the Mount, "When you fast ... do it this way." He is not instructing us to fast, but if we are going to engage in fasting then we should do it in a way that does not cater to the ego. He explains: "When you fast, do not look somber as the hypocrites do, for they disfigure their faces to show others they are fasting. Truly I tell you, they have received their reward in full. But when you fast, put oil on your head and wash your face, so that it will not be obvious to others that you are fasting...."

The real issue is not eating but ego. Jesus is speaking about fasting from ego. The point is not whether or not we fast, but how we do it. If we fast, no one should know we are doing it. If people know we are fasting, it feeds the ego. What good is starving the body to feed the ego? If we are going to engage in any spiritual practice, we are to do it without ego. This is a general principle throughout Jesus' teaching on spiritual practices. Spiritual disciplines must originate from the Spirit – the True Self – and not the egoic self, which is the false self.

The last of the spiritual disciplines that Jesus addresses in the Sermon on the Mount concerns money and possessions. Jesus returns to this topic often in his teachings, so it seems to be important to him. He says in the Sermon on the Mount: "Do not store up for yourselves treasures on earth, where moths and vermin destroy, and where thieves break in and steal. But store up for yourselves treasures in heaven, where moths and vermin do not destroy, and where thieves do not break in and steal. For where your treasure is, there your heart will be also."

How far Christians have strayed from the teachings of Jesus! These days megachurch pastors are multi-millionaires. How unchristlike! Some preachers proclaim a prosperity gospel that is the exact opposite of what Jesus modeled and taught. Jesus told the rich young ruler to sell all that he had and give to the poor and come follow him. When the man couldn't do it, Jesus turned to his disciples and said, "It is harder for a rich man to enter the Kingdom of God than for a camel to go through the eye of a needle."

In the Gospel of Luke's version of the Sermon on the Mount, Jesus does not say "Blessed are the poor in spirit"; he says simply "blessed are the poor." To stress his point he adds some woes to go along with the blessings. He says, "Woe to you who are rich, for you have already received your comfort." Yet Christians ignore these teachings of Jesus. It boggles the mind how deep in darkness Christians can be and not even know it! Jesus addresses this spiritual blindness in this section. He says next: "The eye is the lamp of the body. If your eyes are healthy, your whole body will be full of light. But if your eyes are unhealthy, your whole body will be full of darkness. If then the light within you is darkness, how great is that darkness!"

This is all about spiritual sight. When you see Reality as it is ... when you see the Kingdom of God, the One, the All, and that All is One – then you see everything clearly by its light. But if you can't see this, then you are spiritually blind – no matter how rigorous you are in your spiritual practices and observances.

Jesus tells us to fast from possessions. Jesus says, "Do not store up for yourselves treasures on earth, where moths and vermin destroy, and where thieves break in and steal. But store up for yourselves treasures in heaven, where moths and vermin do not destroy, and where thieves do not break in and steal. For where your treasure is, there your heart will be also."

Americans – including American Christians - value wealth highly. It is the American Dream to become rich. Yet Jesus warns us continually about the dangers of being rich. Jesus says here in this section, "No one can serve two masters. Either you will hate the one and love the other, or you will be devoted to the one and despise the other. You cannot serve both God and money." The New Testament repeatedly says money is dangerous. The First Epistle to Timothy says, "The love of money is the root of all evil." You will not hear that preached often in churches.

There is nothing wrong or unspiritual about having adequate food, shelter, clothing, and healthcare. It is natural to want enough to be safe and healthy. But beyond the physical needs is where ego comes in. The ego stores up more and more wealth and possessions in order to build a cocoon around itself. "Building bigger barns" is how Jesus describes it in one parable. The ego tries to protect itself with wealth. It identifies with its possessions. A loss of possessions feels like a loss of oneself.

The truth is just the opposite. Possessions are an extension of the ego. And like the ego they are not real. It is an illusion that we can own anything. In truth we do not own anything. That includes the body and the self, even though we refer to them as "our body" and "ourselves."

When these attachments to the physical are seen as futile, then we glimpse what we really are. We are not a thing, and we can own no things. To be attached to things is to be lost. For that reason Jesus recommends that we store up treasures in heaven, not treasures on earth.

Unfortunately that phrase "treasures in heaven" has been badly misinterpreted by Christianity. We have turned eternal life into something we can possess, rather than something we are. Religion becomes a transactional mechanism to own eternal life for oneself. It becomes something we have and that others do not have. That makes us feel special and boosts the ego. Heaven is turned into an ego's paradise - a private, gated retirement community.

The apostle Paul fed that illusion with unhelpful metaphors, such as the passage in First Corinthians where he talks about building on a foundation using gold, silver, costly stones, wood, hay or straw. Christians imagine themselves sending building materials up to heaven during their lifetime, so that when they arrive after death they will have a heavenly mansion fully furnished waiting for them.

We have simply exchanged worldly riches for a concept of spiritual riches that will make us big shots in heaven. Dante's Divine Comedy pictures levels in heaven, which appeal to the ego. Heaven becomes all about a separate little self having its own little heavenly kingdom. It is all ego.

This is not what Jesus is talking about when he speaks of spiritual riches! For Jesus the Kingdom of Heaven not a place in the sky where we build a mansion funded by a spiritual IRA that will ensure a prosperous eternal retirement. Jesus is talking about getting rid of the whole idea of the self and possessions.

We own nothing now. Everything is on loan from God. We do not own our bodies, even though we call them ours. We own nothing because we are nothing. There is no separate psychological entity – no self - to own anything. Possessions are an illusion of the self. Fasting from ego is reveals that we are nothing and own nothing. When we see we are nothing, then we paradoxically see we are the All.

The Gospel of Thomas begins with Jesus saying: "Let him who seeks continue seeking until he finds. When he finds, he will become troubled. When he becomes troubled, he will be astonished, and he will rule over the All." That All is spiritual riches. To not know this All is true poverty. Jesus says right after that verse: "But if you will not know yourselves, you dwell in poverty and it is you who are that poverty." Spiritual riches is to know the truth and be set free from the illusion of the ego and its possessions.

Learning from Nature How to Live

In this chapter I examine one of the most beautiful passages in the Bible, sometimes known as the "lilies of the field" passage. The topic of this section is worry or anxiety. Jesus just finished talking about the danger of wealth and possessions. Now he delves deeper. He goes beyond unhealthy obsession with money to more ordinary financial concerns. He talks about the very natural fear of not having enough food to eat. This is called "food insecurity" these days.

That was a very real issue for people living in an agrarian society in the first century. People were completely dependent on circumstances beyond their control: weather, droughts, floods, pestilence, and invading armies. Any of these could cause a famine, which was a regular and real danger in those days. When we read the Bible, we see that a lot of the Bible deals with that reality. It is still a reality today. Lots of people deal with hunger and homelessness now.

Jesus does not tell us how to solve that serious problem of extreme poverty, although he already mentioned giving to those in need as a spiritual discipline. Here he addresses the fear we might have about not having the essentials of life. This would also apply to worrying about how we are going to pay the bills: the mortgage, the rent, the utilities, the grocery bills, and clothing. It is a very real daily concern for many people.

You might be worried about these matters right now. How do we deal with this scary situation in a spiritual manner that is consistent with Jesus' teaching about the Kingdom of God? Jesus' answer is to learn from nature. Specifically he mentions the birds of the air and the flowers of the field. He says:

Therefore I tell you, do not worry about your life, what you will eat or drink; or about your body, what you will wear. Is not life more than food, and the body more than clothes? Look at the birds of the air; they do not sow or reap or store away in barns, and yet your heavenly Father feeds them. Are you not much more valuable than they? Can any one of you by worrying add a single hour to your life?

And why do you worry about clothes? See how the flowers of the field grow. They do not labor or spin. Yet I tell you that not even Solomon in all his splendor was dressed like one of these. If that is how God clothes the grass of the field, which is here today and tomorrow is thrown into the fire, will he not much more clothe you— you of little faith?

Do flowers worry? Do birds worry? I plant flowers around my house. I don't know much about horticulture. I could not tell you the name of many of the flowers in my yard, but I enjoy them. My wife loves feeding the birds, as well as the other wild animals that visit our home. We have many opportunities to meditate on flowers of the field, the birds of the air and the animals of the forest. These creatures are our spiritual teachers.

Jesus directs our attention to these spiritual teachers of the natural world. He points out that they do not worry. The flowers around our house do not worry. The birds do not worry. The fox, bears, possums, raccoons, and moose that visit our yard do not worry. The stray cat that comes to our door daily for food does not worry. They live and die without worry. Yet we worry. Why?

We worry because we are humans. Humans have a personal self-conscious self. I would ordinarily use the word ego here. But I am often misunderstood when I use the word ego. Many people understand the word in the psychological sense as a particular part of the human psyche. When I use the word ego I am not speaking psychologically. I use "ego" to refer to the whole psyche, which is the Greek word used in the New Testament for self. Ego is the Greek word for I – the sense of personal self-identity. That is how I use the term.

Humans worry because we think we are an individual personal self that is separate from the world. This self-consciousness is what distinguishes humans from lilies, sparrows and possums. With this separate identity comes a sense of time and the ability to think about the future, which flowers and birds don't do. With the idea of a future comes the thought that the future may not provide enough for us to live. That brings worry.

To repeat, we worry because we are human. The solution to worrying is to transcend our human identity. Not identify with the human ego and body. The cure for anxiety is to go beyond the human self – the human psyche. This does not mean becoming less than human, but more than human. It means seeing what we really are.

Teilhard de Chardin is credited with the oft-repeated quote: "We are not human beings having a spiritual experience. We are spiritual beings having a human experience." First of all, it is not clear that Teilhard actually said those words. In any case I would modify it to say: We are not humans having a spiritual experience but Spirit having a human experience.

We are the One Spirit, the World Soul, manifesting as humans. We are Being expressed as human beings. Humans are zoologically apes that have evolved to have a slightly larger brain and cerebral cortex than other primates. This accounts for the development of the sense of a separate personal self. Yet in reality we are the same Spirit that animates all living things, including the birds of the air and the lilies of the field. The key to freedom from worry, anxiety and all the other self-created forms of suffering is to rediscover what we really are. We rediscover what we have in common with other living things.

What we have in common is life. At the core we are the same Life that animates all living things. This is Divine Life. The prologue of John's Gospel says of Christ: "In him was Life, and that Life was the Light of men." This Life can be called other names. We can call it intelligence. We can call it consciousness, although I find I am also misunderstood when I use that term. Awareness is another word that is useful in pointing to this Life. We can also call it the Divine or Spirit.

Call this whatever you want, as long as you recognize what I am pointing to with these words. The Essence of our human nature is the essence of all living things and the Essence of the Universe. When we shift our sense of identity from these tiny human psyches and bodies to the cosmic Universal Awareness, then worry falls away. Birds and lilies embody Divine Life effortlessly and without a sense of self to fight against it. That is why they do not worry. Jesus points to our fellow creatures on this planet and suggests that we learn from them.

Jesus ends the section saying: "So do not worry, saying, 'What shall we eat?' or 'What shall we drink?' or 'What shall we wear?' For the pagans run after all these things, and your heavenly Father knows that you need them. But seek first his kingdom and his righteousness, and all these things will be given to you as well. Therefore do not worry about tomorrow, for tomorrow will worry about itself. Each day has enough trouble of its own."

To counter the tendency to worry, Jesus suggests that we seek the Kingdom of God, which is Nondual awareness. He tells us to live in the Now. Live in today and not in tomorrow. Tomorrow is just a thought in the mind which gives rise to worry. Take one day at a time, he says. Or as my wife said to a young man suffering from addiction which we picked up hitching-hiking the other day: Take one hour at the time, one minute at a time, one second at a time. When we do that there is no time to worry.

Do Not Judge

This section of the Sermon on the Mount is one of the greatest, as well as one of the most misused, teachings of Jesus. It is about judging. It has its roots in Jesus' teaching of nonduality. Jesus says:

Judge not, that you be not judged. For with what judgment you judge, you will be judged; and with the measure you use, it will be measured back to you. And why do you look at the speck in your brother's eye, but do not consider the plank in your own eye? Or how can you say to your brother, 'Let me remove the speck from your eye'; and look, a plank is in your own eye? Hypocrite! First remove the plank from your own eye, and then you will see clearly to remove the speck from your brother's eye.

There was a study done by Barna Research group about a decade ago. It surveyed Americans ages 16-29 years old to discover what they thought of Christians and churches, presumably to understand why so many in this group were leaving the church. The result was a book entitled "unChristian: What a New Generation Really Thinks about Christianity...and Why It Matters." It revealed that this age group's perceptions of Christianity was overwhelmingly negative. The three most common perceptions of Christianity were that

Christians are anti-homosexual, judgmental, and hypocritical, in that order.

This judgmental attitude is what Jesus is addressing in the Sermon on the Mount. Jesus did not judge. He never had a harsh word to say about those who were labeled "sinners" by the religious culture of his day. That contrasts with today, when many Christians define themselves by what and whom they are against. Jesus had a lot to say about judgmental religious people. Jesus' most common accusation was that they were hypocritical. It is sad that 2000 years later those who profess to follow Jesus are the ones who are doing exactly what Jesus speaks against.

Jesus' words are rooted in nonduality. Judgment and its cousin condemnation are rooted in a dualistic way of looking at the world. The only way that you can judge is by separating and dividing. Only then can one judge. If all is seen as one, then one does not judge. We judge someone only if we see them as different from us. Different is dangerous in dualistic thinking. To label someone as different often leads to thinking they are worse, or at least their behavior is worse than ours.

This is ego. Ego is blind to nondual reality. The truth is that we are no better than the one we are judging. Not only are we no better, but we are no different from the one we are judging. I and the other are one. By judging others we are actually judging ourselves. As the saying goes, when you point a finger at another person, you are pointing three fingers at yourself. Judgment produces guilt and shame in us, either consciously or unconsciously. That in turn causes all sorts of problems, both personal and societal.

The other day I was reading a "letter to the editor" from a New Hampshire state representative in our local newspaper. It was an example of self-righteous judgment and hypocrisy. The letter was given the title: 'Take kids out of schools, which are following path of Hitler." The representative compared Democrats to Adolf Hitler, Vladimir Lenin, and Joseph Stalin. He said that Democrats are trying to turn public schools into training centers for Hitler Youth. It was a horrible letter, which said much more about the writer than anyone else.

The writer could have made his case about education reform and parental rights without all the moralistic and partisan rhetoric, and people would have listened to him. I would have listened to him. God knows we need to improve American education! Yet all he did was divide people. His attitude was so condescending and arrogant, that even if you were sympathetic to his viewpoint on the issues, you wouldn't want anything to do with him or any bill he might propose.

This man does not realize that he is no different than his enemy. He is unwilling to take the plank out of his own eye. He is so blind that he does not even notice there is a plank in his eye. The reality is that his position would not exist without the opposing position. That is why American politics has produced a two party system and not a three or four or five party system. We tend toward dualism. We need an opponent in order to reinforce our egoic identity. Enemies create each other.

You would not know what right is without wrong. Good cannot exist without evil. Freedom could not exist without bondage. Negative cannot exist without positive. There is no up without down, no high without low, no light without darkness. All dualities are actually one whole that includes the two opposing sides. A coin cannot have a front without a back, yet together they are one. That is the case with all duality. You cannot have magnet without two poles. You cannot have a battery without a positive and negative terminal. A bird cannot fly without two wings.

What appears as opposing dualities is actually nonduality. Nondual Reality includes all dualities. When one sees the unity at the heart of reality, then one sees that it includes all opposites. That is the meaning of the Yin Yang symbol.

The ego does not see that. It needs to be the good guy who is opposed to the bad guy. That means somebody has to play the bad guy. Egos need enemies. For us to be as righteous as we can be, our enemies have to be as unrighteous as they can be. Hence the political rhetoric of comparing our enemies to the arch-villains of history.

This is true on both sides of the political spectrum in the United States. Progressives play the dualistic game as much as Conservatives.

Progressives think that conservatives are evil. Progressives compare Republicans to fascists and Nazis. They have to make the opposing party into fascists and Nazis in order to feel like they are in the right. Both parties engage in dualistic thinking. Both sides demonize the other side.

I recently received a comment on a video, entitled "Christianity and Nonduality," accusing me of being Satanic and demonic. The comment read: *"Marshall Davis, you are bringing in the teachings of the pagans and satanist devil-worshiper & through them the devil."* This person has to see me as being in league with the devil in order to consider himself on the side of the angels.

The scribes and Pharisees said the same things about Jesus. They said, "He is possessed by Beelzebul," "He has an unclean spirit," and "by the prince of demons he casts out the demons." Jesus predicted that his followers would be called the same things. He said, "A disciple is not above his teacher, nor a servant above his master. It is enough for a disciple to be like his teacher, and a servant like his master. If the head of the house has been called Beelzebul, how much more the members of his household!"

Religious people – especially in Western religions – see the world as a battleground between good and evil. God is good, and the Devil is evil. The spiritual life is pictured as a war between the forces of light and the forces of darkness, between good and evil. The good feel the need to judge evil and destroy evil. They turn God into a Judge and are glad to do God's work of judging on earth. That is the source of religious persecution and violence.

Kipling wrote, "East is east and west is west and never the twain shall meet." In nonduality the twain not only meet, they are two sides of the same reality. Nondual Reality includes both good and evil. The God beyond God - the True God, the Ground of Being, Being Itself, the One Nondual Reality - transcends and includes the duality of good and evil.

This is very difficult for those of us nurtured in Christianity to accept. We are used to thinking in terms of a God of Light that is at war with the god of darkness, who is "the god is this world." But Jesus says in the Sermon on the Mount, "Resist not evil" or "Resist not an evil one." That sounds like heresy to Christian ears. Christianity understands itself as resisting evil.

The Letter to the Ephesians compares a Christian to a Roman soldier putting on the "full armor of God" and with the shield of faith resisting "all the fiery darts of the evil one." The Book of Revelation pictures history as a cosmic battle between the forces of good and evil. Jesus is literally pictured as the good guy with a sword riding on a white horse slaying the forces of evil. That is not the Jesus of the Sermon on the Mount. Jesus says, "Do not resist one who is evil."Jesus did not come into Jerusalem on a white horse with a sword; he came on a donkey with palm fronds.

The Way of Jesus makes no sense to traditional dualistic religion, politics, war, or national policy. But Jesus is not talking about those social causes. He is talking about spirituality. Spiritual awakening reveals that ultimately there is no duality. We wake up to see that we are our enemy. We include both evil and good, right and wrong in ourselves. When we take the plank out of our own eye, we step back and say "Wow! How did I never see that before?"

When we realize that we are the whole and not one half fighting the other half, it undercuts the tendency to judge others. We realize that when we judge others we are actually judging ourselves, because they are our selves. It is the height of hypocrisy to condemn people as being so different from us that we have to kill them to rid the world of evil.

This teaching of nonduality is difficult for people to see and accept. When we voice this approach people think we are surrendering to evil, collaborating with evil, or secretly on the side of the demons. We are viewed as dangerous. That is why Jesus follows up this teaching with these words. He says, "Do not give what is holy to the dogs; nor cast your pearls before swine, lest they trample them under their feet, and turn and tear you in pieces." He is cautioning us about how to speak about this nondual truth. He is saying, "This is holy. So be careful how you speak it and to whom you speak it. Because people will not understand, and they will attack you for it."

Comparing people to dogs and swine would be condescending and judgmental coming from anyone but Jesus. Yet in Jesus' mouth it is wisdom. He is saying that the gospel of nonduality is so radical that we have to be careful how we speak it. This is why Jesus spoke to the crowds in parables, but explained parables privately to his closest disciples. This is the radical gospel of Christian nonduality.

How to Enter the Kingdom of God

The Sermon on the Mount focuses on entering the Kingdom of God. From a Buddhist perspective this question would be expressed as how to enter Nirvana or how to be enlightened. The Hindu might ask how to be liberated. Different spiritual traditions use different terms for this, but it is the same spiritual reality.

Jesus addresses this topic elsewhere in his teachings as well. For example in the Gospel of John Jesus says that one has to be born again to enter the Kingdom of God. Jesus is not talking about the evangelical conversion experience. Jesus is talking about spiritual sight. He says to Nicodemus during that famous conversation, "Unless one is born again, he cannot see the Kingdom of God."

Jesus calls this being "born from above" or "born anew" or "born of the Spirit." His metaphor of rebirth is meant to convey that spiritual awakening is like entering a new world. Jesus experienced this transformation at his baptism. To enter the Kingdom of God is to enter into an entirely new way of seeing. It is a shift in perspective.

The million dollar question is "How?" How does one enter the Kingdom of God, the Realm of God, or the Spiritual Realm? Jesus answers, "Ask, and it will be given to you; seek, and you will find; knock, and it will be opened to you. For everyone who asks receives, and the one who seeks finds, and to the one who knocks it will be opened." In other words it is as simple as asking. The best translation of the Jesus' words is "keep on asking, keep on seeking, and keep on knocking."

Jesus is stressing the quality of persistence or perseverance. He teaches this in other parables, such as the widow who wouldn't stop asking the unjust judge for justice. Or the woman who kept looking for the coin she had lost until she found it. Or the shepherd who kept searching for the lost sheep until he found it. The most important quality of the spiritual life is persistence or perseverance.

This takes dedication. The spiritual quest is not a pastime, a game or a hobby. It consumes you completely. I can testify that this is true in my life. All my adult life I have had a hunger and thirst for truth. I did not stop until I found what I was looking for, even though it took me forty years. We see that determination in the story of the Buddha. After years of seeking and trying different spiritual disciplines, Gautama decided to sit down under a tree. He said that he would not arise until he was enlightened or dead. Life or death determination that is the key.

Skepticism is an important part of that determination. Near the end of my search I was deconstructing my Christianity. I carefully investigated every aspect of my Christian faith to see if what I had believed for decades was really true. I was relentless in my skepticism. I was persistent. This final stage took two and a half years, but I did not stop. I was ruthless in my search. I would accept no easy answers.

The problem is that most people are not willing to look beyond the conventional solutions. They are too willing to accept the easy pre-packaged religious answers offered by preachers and teachers. They get tired of looking after a while, and they settle for religion rather than truth. Truth is not a religion, a theology or a philosophy. Those are substitutes for truth. If you persevere – no matter how long it takes or what the consequences – then you find.

Jesus also says that we are to expect to find what we are looking for. This is not a hopeless search. In Christian language, we are to have faith that we will be given what we are asking for. Then the door will open. Jesus says, "Which one of you, if his son asks him for bread, will give him a stone? Or if he asks for a fish, will give him a serpent? If you then, who are evil, know how to give good gifts to your children, how much more will your Father who is in heaven give good things to those who ask him!" in the Gospel of Luke Jesus says, "give the Holy Spirit to those who ask." In other words if you are persistent, your prayers will be answered. You will find. Do not give up hope.

Persistence and faith. We ask, and seek, and knock in hope. We expect to find if we do not give up. That hope is what keeps us asking, seeking, and knocking long after others have given up and settled. We have faith and hope because we trust what Jesus says about the Kingdom of God.

What does he say about the Kingdom? He says the Kingdom of God is not far away. It is within you. Pharisees came to Jesus asking where the Kingdom of God is and when it would come. Jesus replied, "The coming of the kingdom of God is not something that can be observed, nor will people say, 'Here it is,' or 'There it is,' because the kingdom of God is within you." This can be also translated "in your midst" meaning "you are in the middle of it, it is all around you."

In the Gospel of Thomas, Jesus says, "If those who lead you say to you, 'See, the kingdom is in the sky,' then the birds of the sky will precede you. If they say to you, 'It is in the sea,' then the fish will precede you. Rather, the kingdom is inside of you, and it is outside of you. When you come to know yourselves, then you will become known, and you will realize that it is you who are the sons of the living father." Jesus said, "Split a piece of wood, and I am there. Lift up the stone, and you will find me there."

In other words, what you are seeking is already here now. The Truth you are seeking is all around you. You are in the Kingdom of God, and it is in you. You are already enlightened. You already have eternal life. That is the paradox of spiritual truth. There is nowhere we have to go and nothing we have to do to enter the Kingdom of Heaven. It is simply a matter of realizing what is here now. Realizing who we are here now. The Kingdom of Heaven is at hand. All we have to do is notice it is at our fingertips.

It is that simple. Because it is so simple, it is often missed. We keep knocking, and then one day we realize that the door is open, and it has always been open. There is a famous painting of Christ knocking on a door, usually interpreted as the door of the human heart. When you look closely at the paining, you see that there is no handle or latch on the outside of the door. That is because it can only be opened from the inside. There is no bondage except self-bondage. There is no separation besides self-separation.

Duality puts up walls and closed doors to distinguish inside from outside, us from God. But if God is truly omnipresent, there can be no inside or outside. I recently heard a guy joking that his house was so small that the front door is the back door. We knock on the door of the Kingdom of God, and when it opens, it opens to where we already are. Inside is outside. We do not have to go anywhere. Here and now is the Kingdom of God.

It is so simple. Yet it appears so difficult. Jesus explores this paradox in his next words where he gives a further teaching on how to enter the Kingdom of God. How do we enter the Kingdom of God? Jesus says, "Enter by the narrow gate. For the gate is wide and the way is easy that leads to destruction, and those who enter by it are many. For the gate is narrow and the way is hard that leads to life, and those who find it are few."

Enter by the narrow gate. The word "narrow" does not adequately communicate what Jesus means. The old King James Version of the Bible translates it better, but it uses a world rarely heard today. It renders it, "Enter ye in at the strait gate: for wide is the gate, and broad is the way, that leadeth to destruction, and many there be which go in thereat: Because strait is the gate, and narrow is the way, which leadeth unto life, and few there be that find it."

The gate is strait. Not straight as in a straight line, meaning not curvy. It is strait as in straitjacket. It is so strait that you can't move. You certainly cannot bring anything with you through that narrow gate. When a rich young man asked Jesus how to inherit eternal life, Jesus said, "It is harder for a rich man to enter the Kingdom of God than for a camel to go through the eye of a needle." You cannot bring anything with you. Not possessions and certainly not the ego.

There is a tourist sight in New Hampshire called Polar Caves, located about an hour's drive from where we live. In those caves is a passage called the Lemon Squeeze. It is so tight that you have to squeeze through the passageway. Children can fit through, but people my size cannot fit through it.

That is what Jesus is saying about the way to the Kingdom of God. You have to squeeze through. It is strait. You can't take anything with you through it. Not your backpack of self-identity. Not your racial, ethnic, sexual or religious identity. Not your religion. Not your religious baggage filled with doctrines. Not your church. Not your beliefs. Not your worldview. Not your politics. You have to leave all that behind. With every step you take through this narrow way, you leave something more behind until there is nothing left. That is why Jesus likens it to rebirth. It I like pushing through the birth canal. When you let go of everything, and you are nothing, then you see the Kingdom of God. You enter the Kingdom of God.

Most people – like the rich young man that Jesus met - are not willing to do that. They can't "bring themselves" do it. They choose the broad way, the way of popular religion, where millions believe they can have their cake and eat it too. There are lots of preachers who will sell you this cheap grace. Jesus says this the broad way that leads to destruction. The narrow way is life. Historically only a few take this road less traveled. Religions and spiritual communities tend to form around the spiritual pioneers who take the "road not taken," to use the paradoxical title of Frost's poem. Yet anyone can enter, if they are willing to pay the price. All it costs is everything.

Nondual Discernment

Jesus ends his longest and most famous teaching by warning us to be careful of those who would misinterpret his teachings to promote their own agenda. In other words, he advises us to use discernment when it comes to spiritual teachers.

At first glance discernment may appear to be a dualistic activity. It distinguishes one from another, which are two. Yet in reality all is one; the false teacher and true teacher are both expressions of one reality. Yet some teachers point to the nondual Kingdom of God better than others. That is what Jesus is speaking about in this section. I am calling it nondual discernment.

Jesus uses a series of metaphors to warn us about those who would distort his message of the Holy Reality, which he calls the Kingdom of God. First he uses the famous metaphor of a wolf in sheep's clothing. He says, "Beware of false prophets, who come to you in sheep's clothing but inwardly are ravenous wolves." Prophet is another word for spiritual teacher. Some teachers appear harmless, but in reality they are dangerous.

My wife and I are watching the new season of the Hulu series *Reservation Dogs*. The episode we viewed last night took place in one of the infamous Indian Training Schools, which were known for the abuse of indigenous children.

Unfortunately many of these schools were run by Christians. In this case the school was run by Catholic nuns. The closing scene zeroed in on the gravestone of one of the children named Little Bird. Under his name it read: "Killed by human wolves." That is the metaphor that Jesus used. Some religious leaders are human wolves. It is best to keep your distance from them.

There are true spiritual teachers and false ones. Jesus is instructing us to use discernment when it comes to spiritual leaders. Jesus specifically had in mind people like the Pharisees, Sadducees, scribes, teachers of the law, and chief priests of his day. They considered themselves to be guardians of divine truth. Yet they ended up banding together to have Jesus executed for teaching the truth. They were wolves in sheep's clothing. The sad thing is that they did not even know they were wolves. They thought they were protecting people from Jesus, whom they considered a blasphemer.

Unfortunately that is exactly the situation we find in Christianity today. Many leaders in Christianity today speak against the original message of Christ and consider it blasphemy. The original nondual message of Jesus has been transformed by Christian leaders into a dualistic religion called Christianity. This pattern happens in all establishment religion: Christianity, Islam, Judaism, Hinduism, Buddhism, or any other ism.

There is the message of the Lamb, the One Nondual Reality, and there is the message of the wolf. The fox is guarding the henhouse in

Christianity today, to use another metaphor. The lamb is on the cross, and the wolf is on the throne. Jesus instructs us to discern one from the other. Pay attention when religious leaders get too close to the throne. They are court prophets; they are false prophets, wolves in sheep's clothing.

The second metaphor Jesus uses is fruit trees. Jesus says, "You will recognize them by their fruits. Are grapes gathered from thornbushes, or figs from thistles? So, every healthy tree bears good fruit, but the diseased tree bears bad fruit. A healthy tree cannot bear bad fruit, nor can a diseased tree bear good fruit. Every tree that does not bear good fruit is cut down and thrown into the fire. Thus you will recognize them by their fruits."

How do we discern true spiritual teachers from false? Jesus says that the surest way is to examine the fruit. Teachers who are infatuated with money, sex, and power are wolves in sheep's clothing. If a church, denomination, or spiritual community is involved in scandals involving sexual misconduct and financial wrongdoing, then you can be sure it is rotten to the root. If it is involved in cover-ups and deception, there is disease at the core. It is not a healthy tree. If a leader is always asking for money, that person is serving Mammon, not God. It doesn't matter if the person is a megachurch pastor or a Hindu guru. Bad fruit indicates a rotten tree.

Jesus goes on to remind us that it does not matter if leaders profess to follow Jesus or if their ministry is accompanied by miracles. Every religion has their miracles. The court magicians of Pharaoh's court imitated the miracles of Moses. Truth is not about special effects. It is about consciously living as an expression of God. It is about walking in the Way, the Tao of Christ. Jesus says, "Not everyone who says to me, 'Lord, Lord,' will enter the kingdom of heaven, but the one who does the will of my Father who is in heaven. On that day many will say to me, 'Lord, Lord, did we not prophesy in your name, and cast out demons in your name, and do many mighty works in your name?' And then will I declare to them, 'I never knew you; depart from me, you workers of lawlessness.'"

It doesn't matter how much a person insists they are a true Christian. It doesn't matter if they believe all the right things. It doesn't matter whether they call Jesus, "Lord, Lord!" What matters is whether their lives give evidence of following Jesus. That is why I focus on the teachings and example of Jesus rather than the teachings of later Christianity. The 2000 years of Christian tradition, which has accumulated around the figure of Jesus, matter not one bit. They add nothing to Christ. Creeds and confessions of faith are sideshows. All these ideas, which the church now insists is essential to Christianity, are not essential to being a follower of Jesus.

A few weeks ago the church where we attend received some new members. As part of the initiation ceremony the prospective members stood in front of the congregation. The Apostle's Creed was read, and they had to publicly profess that they believed it. This ancient creed has a lot of stuff in it that Jesus never taught. For example, it says that Jesus was God's only Son, that he was conceived by the Holy Spirit, born of the Virgin Mary, that he descended into hell and ascended into heaven. This creed talks about believing in the holy catholic church, the communion of saints, and the resurrection of the body.

Most Christian churches have some a set of beliefs that members are expected to accept in order to be considered a Christian. These doctrines are listed in catechisms, creeds and confessions of faith. Yet Jesus did require a person to accept a set of beliefs in order to become his follower. Jesus did not teach or believe most of the doctrines in the Apostles Creed, much less the later creeds, which are much more wordy and elaborate. This is why for the final years I was the pastor of this church I did not require anyone to believe doctrines in order to join the church. I simply invited people to follow Jesus. If that minimal requirement was enough for Jesus, it was good enough for me.

Doctrines and dogma do not add anything to Jesus' message. In fact doctrines take away from it. Requiring people to profess belief in a set of doctrines is like putting a bushel basket over a lamp. It extinguishes the light of Christ. The Kingdom of God is not about beliefs. It is about the Way of Jesus. It is important to discern between secondary doctrines and the core teaching of Jesus Christ.

To end his sermon Jesus uses one final metaphor. "Everyone then who hears these words of mine and does them will be like a wise man who built his house on the rock. And the rain fell, and the floods came, and the winds blew and beat on that house, but it did not fall, because it had been founded on the rock. And everyone who hears these words of mine and does not do them will be like a foolish man who built his house on the sand. And the rain fell, and the floods came, and the winds blew and beat against that house, and it fell, and great was the fall of it."

Jesus is telling us to ground our lives on his words, like a builder building his house on a rock foundation. We stand on the one Rock of Nondual Reality rather than the shifting sands of duality. One of my sons is a carpenter. He builds post-and-beam houses in New Hampshire. He recently built his own timber frame house with lumber cut from his own property. He did all the carpentry himself, but he hired someone to put in the foundation. He made sure it was someone he knew and had worked with, who knew what he was doing. That is because it does not matter how well the house is constructed if the foundation is not solid.

Each spring my wife and I spend a few weeks on the eastern coast of Florida. This year we saw vast damage caused by Hurricane Ian. Up and down our beach we saw beach houses in ruins, which had been destroyed by ocean surges. I talked to one man whose house survived intact, but whose neighbor's house was totaled. He told me the difference was the foundation. When it comes to spiritual teachers we need to use discernment. I have found the words of Jesus to be a firm foundation.

How Christianity Lost Its Way

In this book I have interpreted the Sermon on the Mount from a nondual perspective. Nonduality was the original gospel of Jesus. Jesus proclaimed the Kingdom of God, which is his term for the awareness of the omnipresence of the Divine. His message was the Presence of God, not as a doctrine to be believed but a reality to be experienced. This was the gospel of Jesus. This is not the gospel that has been historically proclaimed by the Christian church. When one looks for evidence of this message throughout church history it is difficult to find.

One can spot glimpses of this nondual gospel sticking up like flowers growing between the cracks in a sidewalk, but it is rare. One sees it in the Deserts Fathers and Mothers, who retreated into the Egyptian desert when the Church became overtly hostile to this message. One sees it in Christian mystics like Meister Eckhart, Julian of Norwich and the anonymous author of the Cloud of Unknowing. One sees it in monks like Brother Lawrence and Thomas Merton.

Early in church history one can see it in the manuscripts of the Nag Hammadi Library. These are ancient Christian texts from the first three centuries that proclaimed this awareness of the Kingdom of God. But in the fourth century these books were banned and ordered to be destroyed by the church. Fortunately a Christian community in Nag Hammadi, Egypt, disobeyed the Church's instruction. They buried their manuscripts in a cave, and they were recovered in the 20th century. This library includes books like the Gospel of Thomas, which is as ancient as any gospel in the New Testament and reflective of the actual teachings of Jesus of Nazareth.

These texts show that Christianity could have become a movement that preached and lived the firsthand direct awareness of the presence of God. Instead it became a religion of doctrines and legalism. It became a hierarchical institution that replaced experience with dogma and replaced direct awareness of God with obedience to the authority of Church leaders. The gospel of the historical Jesus became a gospel about the Christ of faith, invented by men who did not know Jesus, who did not hear him preach, and who did not experience or understand what Jesus was talking about.

Christianity lost its way. How did this happen? Some think this happened with the rise of Roman Catholicism, the conversion of the Roman emperor Constantine, and the establishment of Christianity as the official religion of the empire. But that was only the final nail in the coffin. Some cite the later Protestant Reformation or Calvinism, or Rationalism, or Fundamentalism. I see the problem beginning much earlier in the history of Christianity. It began before the New Testament was canonized.

I place the blame on the earliest church leaders in the first century. Soon after the lifetime of Jesus, the leadership of the early Christian community fell to two men, neither of whom were among the original twelve apostles. That is where the problem began. Those two men were James and Paul.

James, the younger brother of Jesus, quickly rose to become the head of the Jerusalem church and the *de facto* head of the Christian movement. For the Jerusalem church having a biological sibling of Jesus as the head of the church became more important than the teachings of Jesus. Perhaps this was because monarchial bloodline was very important in that culture. We see this happening later in Islam in the struggle for leadership after Muhammad's death. That struggle produced the two sect of Sunni and Shia.

After Jesus' departure, the Jerusalem church made Jesus' little brother its leader instead of Peter, who seems to have been Jesus' choice. James was a man who did not believe in Jesus or follow Jesus during Jesus' lifetime. He considered Jesus "out of his mind" according to one gospel story. Yet this man took the reins of the nascent church. We see this struggle for leadership reflected in the Book of Acts as well as in the famous "Rock" passage where Jesus seems to declare Peter as the head of the church. The choice of James over Peter was the first misstep in a long series of mistakes that led the early church away from the teachings of Christ.

The second man is even more important in the history of Christianity. He is Saul of Tarsus, better known as the apostle Paul. Paul is the real founder of the religion that we now call Christianity. Ironically Christ is not the founder of the faith that bears his name. That honor goes to a Pharisee who did not know Jesus and who persecuted the early church. Paul had a dramatic conversion on the road to Damascus, and he soon became the most famous spokesman for the young faith.

Yet Paul never met the historical Jesus or heard him teach. From his epistles, it is clear that Paul was unfamiliar with the teachings of Jesus. He never quotes Jesus in his letters, except for his words at the Last Supper. In the *Acts of the Apostles* Paul quotes an unknown maxim of Jesus ("It is more blessed to give than to receive") that is not found in the canonical gospels. That is the extent of Paul's knowledge of Jesus' teaching.

In his Letter to the Galatians he brags about not receiving his gospel from the original apostles who heard Jesus teach! He said he received his gospel as a direct revelation from God. This is reminiscent of the claims of Joseph Smith, the founder of Mormonism. Paul's gospel, not Jesus' message, became the core of Christianity. In many ways Paul was a religious genius, at least as far as church growth is concerned. He took Christianity from being a tiny Jewish sect to becoming a world religion. If it were not for Paul, Jesus of Nazareth would likely have been only a footnote in history. Paul grew the Church by opening the faith up to

Gentiles and distancing it from Jewish law, rites, and practices.

What about the apostle Peter? Yes, Peter was an important apostle, one of Jesus' inner circle. Yet Peter did not have much influence on the direction of Christianity. The single exception is a scene in the Book of Acts that takes place in the house of the Roman centurion Cornelius. Peter witnesses the Holy Spirit filling this Gentile household, and Peter baptized them. According to Acts Peter had a role in opening up the church to non-Jews. Although one wonders how much this story is Pauline propaganda, because Acts is written by Luke, a disciple of Paul.

In either case Paul himself says in his Letter to the Galatians that Peter backtracked on his attitude toward non-Jews. Peter could not decide if he agreed with James or Paul when it came to the inclusion of Gentiles in the church, even after that vision. Peter was not a decisive leader. The Roman Catholic Church claims Peter as the first bishop of Rome and the first pope, but this is his sole claim to fame. Peter was an important early apostle, but Paul was the star of the show.

Pauline Christianity became the dominant form of Christianity. That is evidenced by how many of his writings were included in the New Testament. With later Pseudo-Pauline writings like the Pastoral Epistles, patriarchal authoritarian took hold of the church. Women were sidelined from leadership roles. Church hierarchy, doctrines and laws became all important.

Some people think I am too hard on Paul. Perhaps I am. There is much about Paul's writings that are beautiful and spiritual. He had a mystical side. Portions of his epistles are among the most insightful in the New Testament. Yet Paul could never overcome his inner Pharisee. He struggled with this all his life. As a result his writings are a mixture of spiritual insight and obsession with law and a transactional understanding of salvation, which became the dominant note of Christianity.

Christianity lost its way, not only because of the writings of Paul, but because the four gospels that were included in the Bible were not written by disciples of Jesus, as any credible New Testament scholar will tell you. Two of them – Luke and Mark – where written by disciples of Paul. The Gospel of Matthew was written by an anonymous Jewish Christian. John's gospel is the only one with any credible connection to an apostle. Yet even this gospel admits in its final chapter that the apostle John was not its author, even though the author used John's testimony as the foundation for his work. Yet only these four gospels made it into the Bible. Other gospels and epistles, which did not adhere to the Pauline version of the gospel, were excluded.

In this way Christianity distanced itself from the teachings of Jesus and lost its way. This all happened in the first three hundred years of church history! When the dust settled, "orthodox" Christianity bore no resemblance to the example and teachings of the carpenter of

Nazareth. The history of Christianity since then has been a repetition and expansion of these mistakes of the early centuries.

What can be done about this? Many people abandon Christianity as hopelessly dualistic and legalistic, and have left the church. I remain in the Christian church, despite its shortcomings. I encourage Christians to work within the church and find Christ there. There are people in churches who are sincerely seeking to follow Jesus. All they need is to rediscover his message. We can help that happen.

Fortunately Jesus' message can still be found in the canonical gospels. A little over a hundred years ago, Bible publishers began to print "red letter" editions of the New Testament. These are Bibles that print the words of Jesus in red ink, to distinguish them from the surrounding narrative. The message of Jesus is found in the red letters. Scholars debate whether Jesus actually spoke all the words attributed to him, but the average reader does not need to worry about that. At least not to start.

The original nondual message of the Kingdom of God, which was proclaimed by Jesus, is still to be found in the Scriptures of the Church. They are still read in worship. His words are still studied in Bible Studies. That is why I remain in the Church. When I preach in churches I proclaim the original message of Jesus. I have no illusions that the Church will change, but some people in the church will hear. That is why I stay in the church and why I call myself a

Christian. Because of Jesus Christ and his message in the Sermon on the Mount.

About the Author

Marshall Davis is an ordained American Baptist minister who has served American Baptist and Southern Baptist churches in New Hampshire, Massachusetts, Pennsylvania, Illinois and Kentucky during his forty year ministry as a pastor.

He holds a Bachelor of Arts degree in Religion from Denison University, as well as Master of Divinity and Doctor of Ministry degrees from the Southern Baptist Theological Seminary, Louisville, Kentucky. He has done sabbatical studies at the Tantur Ecumenical Institute for Theological Research in Jerusalem, Israel; Regent's Park College of Oxford University, Oxford, England; and the Shalem Institute for Spiritual Formation in Washington. D.C.

He has a podcast entitled "The Tao of Christ," a YouTube Channel called "Christian Nonduality" and a blog entitled "Spiritual Reflections." He is the author of several books. Links to these resources can be found at MarshallDavis.us or PastorDavis.com.

Having retired from fulltime pastoral ministry in 2016, nowadays he spends most days with his wife at their 18th century home in a small village in the White Mountains of New Hampshire. There he enjoys the mountains and lakes, vegetable gardening, walking, playing backgammon and cribbage, and watching his grandchildren grow. He writes nearly every day and preaches occasionally at nearby churches.

Other Books by Marshall Davis

Experiencing God Directly: The Way of Christian Nonduality

The Tao of Christ: A Christian Version of the Tao Te Ching

Living Presence: A Guide to Everyday Awareness of God

The Gospel of Nonduality: A Spiritual Interpretation of the Gospel of John

Biblical Nonduality

The Practice of the Presence of God in Modern English by Brother Lawrence, translated by Marshall Davis

The Nondual Gospel of Jesus

Christianity Without Beliefs

Unitive Awareness: Talks on Christian Nonduality

Thank God for Atheists: What Christians Can Learn from the New Atheism

The Seeker's Journey: A Contemporary Retelling of Pilgrim's Progress

What Your Pastor Won't Tell You (But I Can Because I'm Retired)

Understanding Revelation

The Evolution of Easter: How the Historical Jesus Became the Risen Christ

The Parables of Jesus: American Paraphrase Version

The Baptist Church Covenant: Its History and Meaning

A People Called Baptist: An Introduction to Baptist History & Heritage

The Gospel of Solomon: The Christian Message in the Song of Solomon

Esther